Cambridge Elements ≡

Elements in Historical Theory and Practice
edited by
Daniel Woolf
Queen's University, Ontario

DEALING WITH DARK PASTS

A European History of Autocritical Memory in Global Perspective

Itay Lotem
University of Westminster

CAMBRIDGE
UNIVERSITY PRESS

Shaftesbury Road, Cambridge CB2 8EA, United Kingdom

One Liberty Plaza, 20th Floor, New York, NY 10006, USA

477 Williamstown Road, Port Melbourne, VIC 3207, Australia

314–321, 3rd Floor, Plot 3, Splendor Forum, Jasola District Centre,
New Delhi – 110025, India

103 Penang Road, #05–06/07, Visioncrest Commercial, Singapore 238467

Cambridge University Press is part of Cambridge University Press & Assessment,
a department of the University of Cambridge.

We share the University's mission to contribute to society through the pursuit of
education, learning and research at the highest international levels of excellence.

www.cambridge.org
Information on this title: www.cambridge.org/9781009507400

DOI: 10.1017/9781009122948

When citing this work, please include a reference to the DOI: 10.1017/9781009122948

First published 2024

A catalogue record for this publication is available from the British Library

ISBN 978-1-009-50740-0 Hardback
ISBN 978-1-009-11414-1 Paperback
ISSN 2634-8616 (online)
ISSN 2634-8608 (print)

Dealing with Dark Pasts

A European History of Autocritical Memory in Global Perspective

Elements in Historical Theory and Practice

DOI: 10.1017/9781009122948
First published online: November 2024

Itay Lotem
University of Westminster

Author for correspondence: Itay Lotem, i.lotem@westminster.ac.uk

Abstract: Since the end of the Second World War, the political rationale to remember the past has shifted from previous focus on states' victories, as these began commemorating their own historical crimes. This Element follows the rise of 'autocritical memory', or the politics of remembrance of a country's own dark past. The Element explores the idea's gestation in West Germany after the Second World War, its globalisation through initiatives of 'transitional justice' in the 1990s and present-day debates about how to remember the colonial past. It follows different case studies that span the European continent – including Germany, France, Britain, Poland and Serbia – and places these in a global context that traces the circulation of ideas of autocritical memory. Ultimately, as it follows the emergence of demands for social and racial justice, the Element questions the usefulness of memory to achieve the goals many political actors ascribe to it.

Keywords: memory of colonialism, Holocaust memory, global memory, coming to terms with the past, memory activism

ISBNs: 9781009507400 (HB), 9781009114141 (PB), 9781009122948 (OC)
ISSNs: 2634-8616 (online), 2634-8608 (print)

Contents

Introduction

In October 2000, the then Mayor of London Ken Livingstone, a prominent figure of the British left, ignited a minor scandal by suggesting the removal of two plinths from their not-so-prominent-positions on one of the capital's main public spaces, Trafalgar Square. Livingstone argued that the statues of the two colonial generals in question, Havelock and Napier, meant nothing to contemporary Londoners, as nobody 'had a clue' who they were.[1] Only twenty years later, this same argument would have seemed bizarre to British protesters, who targeted statues of colonial figures. This was the case in June 2020 in Bristol, as crowds toppled the statues of the slave trader Edward Colston in a demonstration triggered by the global outrage over the murder of George Floyd, a Black man, by a police officer in the US.[2] For these activists, and the national audience that followed the ensuing 'statue controversy' as it developed in the media, contesting symbols of Britain's colonial history regardless of their meaning to the general public had become a political rationale in and of itself. For them, contesting imperial history had become a tool in broader struggles against racism and for racial justice. This development reflected the global rise of memory as a political value. Different actors mobilised history in the name of struggles for 'justice' for their contemporaries.

This Element is about the rise of the phenomenon of *autocritical memory*, rather than *memory* in the general sense, where societies face – or are expected to face – the dark sides of their own history. Autocritical memory is a new phenomenon and differs from any kind of positive memory politics. Celebratory memory has been around for ages, as the commemoration of victories formed political and social identities. Even defeats have been used to strengthen political identities through focus on noble victims who had given their lives for a greater good. The idea, however, of the necessity to deal with a dark past critically and incorporate elements of 'responsibility' into an evolving national identity – and even pride – is a product of the twentieth century and the aftermath of the Second World War. Sociologist Barbara Misztal (2003) has even claimed that coming to terms with the past is the 'grand narrative' of our times.[3] This Element traces the evolvement of this 'grand narrative' from its articulation in (West) Germany after the Second World War to demands for racial justice in the present day.[4] It follows the politicisation of loose ideas of

---

[1] *The Guardian*, 19 October 2000. [2] *The Guardian*, 7 June 2020.
[3] Misztal, *Theories of Social Remembering*.
[4] The Element examines, among other things, the development of memory politics in Germany and some of its present-day challenges. As the Element was drafted in the early months of 2023, it could not address any of the later debates about German memory culture that arose in the aftermath of 7 October 2023.

'facing the past' and 'taking responsibility for crimes' into coherent rationales that informed state action, but also circulated around the globe through a process of borrowing and inspiration. In other words, it asks how the principle of remembering became so politically potent and imbued with so much moral significance in contemporary political cultures, and what is the purpose of all this remembering.

What Is Autocritical Memory?

Memory has become one of the most popular subjects of historical and social enquiry over the last few decades, partly due to scholars' realisation of the impacts of its politicisation. The coining of the term 'collective memory' dates to 1925, to the work of the sociologist Maurice Halbwachs. A student of Durkheim, Halbwachs argued that societies shaped the way individuals understood the world and therefore also defined what they understood and remembered.[5] This tension has since existed between individual memory, which remains a physio-psychological process in the individual human brain, and the understanding of collective memory, where the word itself psychologises society and assumes society can operate as a coherent 'body'. This was particularly apparent in theories that tried to assert how societies 'decide' what is worth 'remembering' and what not. The philosopher Paul Ricoeur, for example, compared social processes of selection to the way individuals rely on the natural qualities of forgetfulness: as people cannot possibly retain all memories, forgetfulness protects the human mind, clearing whatever is considered either unimportant or traumatising.[6] This reflection built on the Freudian concept of *Deckerinnerung*, or 'screen memory', where a child's banal everyday memories substitute painful recollections in the person's consciousness.[7]

The focus on collective memory as a psychologising process ignores the fact that societies cannot 'remember' like the brain. Collective memory is a political process of transmission, omission and interpretation, where different public actors, whom Nancy Wood calls 'vectors of memory',[8] articulate narratives that explain why the past matters to contemporary societies. These actors mobilise history for different reasons that often have little to do with the actual past. They appeal to audiences' emotions to make a case for why society should not only know about what happened in the past but also *care* about it.[9]

---

[5] Halbwachs, *Les cadres sociaux de la mémoire*, 1st Ed., and Halbwachs, *La mémoire collective*, 1st Ed.

[6] See Ricoeur, *La mémoire, l'histoire, l'oubli*. See also Augé, *Les formes de l'oubli*.

[7] See Freud, *Zur Psychopathologie des Alltagslebens*.   [8] Wood, *Vectors of Memory*.

[9] Prochasson, *L'Empire des émotions*.

While many early theoreticians of memory – like the unavoidable Pierre Nora and his *Lieux de mémoire* (places of memory) – assumed the politics of memory was about appealing to collective emotions of pride for the sake of an articulation of a national narrative, this focus changed with the rise of trauma theories in the 1990s and particularly the phenomenon Lea David called 'moral remembrance'.[10] As an increasing number of political and scholarly commentators addressed the longevity and salience of past trauma in the aftermath of conflict, memory became imbued with a moral rationale. Most importantly, interventions became concerned with finding the 'proper' kind of memory that would serve as a vehicle for the articulation of justice for victims. One such theory was Michael Rothberg's influential 'multidirectional memory' that concerned itself at first with the relation between the remembrance of the Holocaust and colonialism.[11] Rothberg condemned the logic of 'real estate' according to which these two memories stood in competition to one another as there was not enough space to address both histories of oppression in the public sphere. To suggest an 'alternative' for 'justice', then, Rothberg assessed different examples of actors that engaged with the past for their 'multidirectionality'. The latter term represented these actors' readiness to create a 'proper' memory that remembered victims of the Holocaust and colonial history in unison and through inspiration rather than conflict. While the theory ticked all moral boxes, its focus on often marginal artistic production as examples of 'proper' memory ignored the actual political landscape in which people mobilised the past for various – and not always noble – priorities. The inspiration between different activists and memory vectors, that Rothberg claimed was a recipe for justice, was often conflictual and violent. More importantly, these exchanges resulted in forms of remembrance that did not suit any model of justice, or 'good' remembrance, yet cannot be de-prioritised by memory scholarship.

Instead of seeking any 'proper' way to remember, this Element is interested in the way memory has become a part of the political discourse for better and for worse. Its main focus is the political rationale of autocritical memory, or the imperative to remember – and reckon with – 'one's own' crimes. In other words, autocritical memory is the establishment of a political process that calls on a polity to integrate its own 'dark past' into its national narrative. As any kind of memory, it involves various levels of narrative formation. Firstly, it relies on a public debate in the form of intellectuals, activists or other political actors, who articulate why it is important for the 'nation' to remember its dark past. Simultaneously, it concerns the ensemble of mechanisms that underpin and perpetuate collective narratives: official commemorations and government pronouncements, continuous public debate, artistic production, education programmes and others.

---

[10] David, *The Past Can't Heal Us.*   [11] Rothberg, *Multidirectional Memory.*

The specificity of autocritical memory in comparison to other theorisations of remembrance of violence lies in the focus on perpetrators rather than victims. The novelty in the emergence of West German memory culture after the Second World War was not only the desire to 'heal' German society and democratise it through remembering the horrors of the war and the Holocaust but also mainly the articulation of a rationale of 'coming to terms' with one's own crimes. This rationale required two elements. The first was a large-scale acceptance of a shared legacy of and national continuity between perpetrators and the new Federal German Republic, rather than continued search of other perpetrators in the form of foreign actors, minority communities or rival political groups. The second was the future-oriented desire to 'move on' and reinvent the identity of former perpetrators. While proponents of autocritical memory shared much of the psychologising and moral approaches that have been described by theorists of multidirectionality or what Lea David calls 'moral remembrance', not least the desire to 'heal' societies, their main preoccupation was not with universality or solidarity with victims. This difference is not only semantic but also explains the social power of early autocritical memory narratives as well as their intellectual horizons. In the same vein, the emergence of autocritical memory as a phenomenon required both widespread intellectual engagement with the necessity of self-introspection and political will to adopt these. In so doing, political actors have inevitably flattened and altered the intellectual meaning assigned to autocriticism.

By addressing the particularity of autocritical memory, this Element explores the intellectual and political trajectories of the concept as well as its transformations. While the memory of glorious victors and of noble victims had always been a part of political processes everywhere, the kind of remembrance that shaped the moral narratives that underpin the current understanding of memory was new. This imperative to 'deal' with one's own crimes began in West Germany after the Second World War. The long process of articulating what 'guilt' and 'responsibility' meant for a West German population that was eager to move on and reintegrate in a new European project coalesced into a political rationale and a model that others then perceived as a success story. The global circulation of this model contributed greatly to the idea of memory as a tool to 'heal' societies rather than just a mechanism that forged identities and belonging. In fact, this model travelled through new international projects of democratisation that perceived German 'success' as a project of reconciliation rather than as a mechanism of internal transformation. In so doing, actors who mobilised remembrance elsewhere claimed to focus on victims and their stories. And yet, remembrance of other people's suffering has never been enough for engagement with moral questions in the societies of perpetrators.[12]

The historical engagement with autocritical memory is thus necessary to complement recent interventions that have questioned the normative acceptance of memory as a tool for 'healing' societies, or what Lea David calls 'moral remembrance'.[13] David in particular questions the inclusion of a victim-centred approach into the toolkit of human rights discourses. Gensburger and Lefranc, simultaneously, argue for rethinking of progressive memory politics beyond 'simple reminding of past', as they provide evidence that learning about crimes did not result in popular identification with victims or with greater acceptance of democratic values.[14] While this Element shares these critiques' main observations and arguments, its main question is how contemporary memory politics have developed from the starting point of autocritical memory, embraced some of its characteristics and changed others.

The German 'model' inspired new actors to embrace 'memory' as a recipe for healing in vastly different contexts, but also as a new political rationale to challenge governments and demand 'dealing with the past' in order to address (and sometimes fix) long-standing issues in contemporary societies, from nationalism to postcolonial racism. In so doing, these actors averted their focus away from understanding perpetrators to centring victim narratives. Yet the questions autocritical memory raises are different than those raised by the moral identification with the victims. Indeed, mobilising the past in Germany after the Second World War or Serbia after the Yugoslav Wars requires facing responsibility for crimes, but also the continuities of social phenomena that enabled these crimes in the first place, whether racism or nationalism. For other actors who then wish to mobilise the past to make demands of descendants of perpetrators to face the crimes of their forebears, it becomes crucial to understand the mechanism of autocritical memory just as much, if not more than that of victim-centred one. Trying to refocus on the meaning of autorictical memory, then, is an attempt to move beyond justified critique of the failings of contemporary memory culture, and instead take stock of its emergence. Returning to the specificities of autocritical memory is an exercise in reassessing what can be salvaged from existing trajectories of memory politics as contemporary societies are facing challenges that require rearticulation of popular narratives and reinvention of memory cultures.

---

[12] Gensburger and Lefranc, *A quoi servent les politiques de mémoire?*

[13] Gensburger and Lefranc, *A quoi servent les politiques de mémoire?*; Baer and Sznaider, *Memory and Forgetting in the Post-Holocaust Era*; David, *The Past Can't Heal Us.*

[14] Gensburger and Lefranc, *A quoi servent les politiques de mémoire?*

Between National and Global: A European History in Global Perspective

Following autocritical memory entails the tracing of the emergence of discourses about responsibility and guilt, as intellectuals, politicians, artists and other public actors tried to make sense of the role of the past for the constitution of contemporary identities. As national state actors appropriated and instrumentalised these discourses, the political rationale of autocritical memory travelled between states and political contexts. However, autocriticism was never the only memory rationale available to actors, who could still choose to interpret history through other approaches: from silence or uninterest in a dark past (which some would then call 'forgetting') to victimhood or straightforward glorification.[15] This Element thus focuses on instances in which actors translated autocritical memory to fit their own political priorities in the present, whether to create more inclusive political identities through Holocaust remembrance or to challenge the state racism through focus on the need to remember colonial history.

Autocritical memory is a 'soft' concept. Nobody has ever claimed to be engaging in autocritical remembrance. Many, however, have used similar sets of arguments to 'deal with the past' through critical self-reflection and often returned to the same success story of the German model, where Germans supposedly had succeeded in 'coming to terms' with their Nazi past. The articulation of what 'dealing with the past' meant in any given place did not occur on a single level of society. While intellectuals formulated narratives about the meaning of history and memory, activists borrowed from academic and intellectual works in their demands for social change, and high-political actors sought to translate these into tangible policy. The interaction between these different actors defined the political uses of the past in any given context. Similarly, actors across national borders addressed similar questions through borrowing from other 'memory actors'.

The concept of autocritical memory thus travelled internationally, but was often articulated on the national level to address national identities and transformations. As memory was an integral part in sustaining the Andersonian 'imagined community' through media attention to national characteristics, autocritical memory became a vehicle for the articulation of new national identities.[16] Writing a history of autocritical memory, even a global one, needs to focus on national cases and on national actors who appropriated this concept differently. In the German inception of autocritical memory, for example, intellectuals and politicians addressed 'dealing with the

---

[15] See, for example, Trouillot, *Silencing the Past.*   [16] Anderson, *Imagined Communities.*

past' as a way to create a new West German identity based on national acceptance of responsibility and the healing power of facing one's own crimes. Even later, critics of Germany's memory culture would target the autocritical model for its lack of inclusiveness and supposed role in hindering the crystallisation of a more globalised German identity (which was, nonetheless, a German identity).

Simultaneously, the concept of autocritical memory has mainly travelled in societies of the Global North, as discourse on national responsibility and coming to terms with crimes became ever more identified with crimes of colonialism and enslavement, in which not only national identities but also broader fields such as 'Europe' or 'the West' are negotiated. For this reason, this Element focuses on the history of autocritical memory on the European continent. For issues of time, scope and coherence, it focuses on national case studies from Europe, whether Germany, France, Serbia, Belgium or the UK, as different actors reappropriated the same concept to address different crimes, whether the Holocaust, the Genocide against Bosniaks or colonial crimes.

The focus on Europe, however, does not assume that Europe was the intellectual centre of such conversations. While responsibility to crimes of the Second World War and colonialism was indeed a European question, the motivation to address issues of responsibility did not always emerge from Europe. Similarly, even as the development of ideas of autocritical memory may have begun in Germany, these quickly developed globally. Ideas of 'transnational justice' that produced trials in the aftermath of the Yugoslav Wars were articulated internationally based on examples not only of Germany but also Argentina and South Africa. Their (non)implementation was also result of outside pressure. Similarly, when national activists in the UK, Germany or Belgium addressed the memory of colonialism in their own countries, they did so through contact with American intellectual literature and activists from the Global South. This Element demonstrates that when European actors engaged in autocritical remembrance, they did so through borrowing and inspiration from other parts of the world and demonstrated that Europe was just one region in a globalised intellectual environment. Focusing on Europe highlights the global dimensions of memory politics with Europe as an interconnected global region. Even as memory debates happened at national level, the 'Andersonian' rationale of defining the nation through shared references borrowed from global debates and interrogations of supranational identities. Actors questioned not only 'who we are as a people' but also 'what does being a global citizen mean'. In other words, what happened in Europe was about European specificities just as much as it related to a global conversation.

The Element's structure represents three phases in the development of auto-critical memory. Section 1 examines the gestation of the concept in two national European contexts in the aftermath of the Second World War. Both in West Germany and in France, political actors developed a national culture of 'coming to terms' with crimes that were now considered as an 'ultimate evil'. In both cases, the gestation of the autocritical model was not in any way given in the direct aftermath of the war, but developed through political struggles. In Germany in particular, however, this model was in no way 'universal', but focused heavily on the rearticulation of German identities after the war. As the memory of the Holocaust quickly became a subject of international interest in the 1990s, however, the so-called German model developed into an example of 'successful dealing with the past'.

This is where Section 2 continues and examines the use of memory within processes of democratisation in Central and Eastern Europe in the 1990s and 2000s following the third wave of democratisation. It begins with the inclusion of memory into the toolkit of 'transitional justice', as international political theorists and decision makers transposed the German 'success' onto a supposedly universal model to successfully deal with transitions into democracy. With the genocidal violence of the 1990s in Rwanda and former Yugoslavia, these same actors then rearticulated the model of transition to adapt it to 'coming to terms' with state crimes through a series of justice mechanisms. The two cases studies of Serbia and Poland thus represent two different Eastern European states that had very different experiences of addressing the past in the process of transition into democracy. In the case of Serbia, this was an immediate post-conflict transition where internal dealing with the memory of the Yugoslav Wars clashed with international demands for change. In the case of Poland, the Jedwabne Debate became a stress test of democratic norms through adoption of autocritical narratives. In both cases, the challenges of autocritical memory and its failure to take a permanent hold reflected the power of narratives of victimisation and the uneasy relationship between dealing with a difficult past and the articulation of future-oriented identities.

Section 3 returns to Western Europe and demonstrates how activists and politicians were able to harness the political rationale of autocritical memory to demand remembering other neglected pasts, and most notably countries' colonial past. While French actors still focused on a French national narrative, however, actors elsewhere redefined memory as a tool for achieving racial justice. Borrowing from debates in the anglophone world and the Global South, they demanded remembrance no longer for the sake of shaping a national consciousness but for the name of transnational fights against racism.

The cases of North-Western European postcolonial activists reflect the challenges of reshaping autocritical narratives to include voices of victims.

1 The Emergence of Autocritical Memory

Before becoming a globalised phenomenon, autocritical memory emerged in the specific context of West Germany in the aftermath of the Second World War, as German intellectuals and politicians grappled with the need to 'come to terms' with the crimes of the Holocaust and the Second World War. This section examines the emergence of the political rationales of autocritical memory in Germany and France as national-specific processes. It follows the intellectuals, activists and politicians who articulated the importance of memory and appropriated it as a component of 'moving on' and creating 'new' German and French national identities that took pride in 'dealing with the past'. In both cases, the political rationale of autocritical memory did not reflect any moral commitment to victims, but a process of reinvention of majority identities in either country.

1.1 Vergangenheitsbewältigung: Out of the Ashes of the War – Immediate Reckoning with the Past in West Germany

Much has been written about the 'German model' of dealing with the past,[17] sometimes as a success story, and at times as a disappointment. Beyond German 'successes' and 'failures' of memory to fight antisemitism and racism, (West) Germany was the laboratory for the articulation of autocritical memory after the defeat in the Second World War. This section will examine the gestation of West German memory culture from debates about guilt and introspection in the late 1940s and 1950s and up to the political articulation of the concept of 'Vergangenheitsbewältigung' (best translated as 'dealing with the past') as one of the pillars of (West) German contemporary identity.[18]

While the 'German model' would later turn into a byword for successful dealing with the past, Germany's immediate post-war circumstance did not seem propitious for critical engagement with the scale of German crimes. Judging by Hannah Arendt's report from the ruins of Berlin in 1950, there was little chance of Germany rising from the ashes of destruction and self-pity, neither as a revived economic powerhouse nor through dealing with the country's past. The exiled Jewish political philosopher returned to the country of her birth from the US and discovered a landscape that was not only in physical ruins

---

[17] David, 'The Emergence of the "Dealing with the Past" Agenda'.

[18] This section focuses on debates in West Germany as the site of articulation of the so-called German model. East German trajectories will appear briefly in Section 3, but otherwise deserve their own attention. For research about East German memory trajectories, see, for example Herf, *Divided Memory*.

but also people who did not offer any sympathy to Jewish suffering beyond the 'deluge of stories about how Germans have suffered'.[19] Arendt's impressions contradict the narrative of 1945 as a 'Stunde Null', or 'hour zero', which incited a reinvention of Germany and Germanness,[20] and suggest there was little popular readiness to assume any responsibility for Nazi crimes. The intellectual and political landscapes of the period also offered some support for Arendt's observations. Intellectuals and politicians created a narrative of 'poor Germany', as they complained that Germans were now turning into 'double victims' of National Socialist takeover and Allied persecution alike.[21] Nonetheless, probably the most defining feature of popular engagement with the immediate past was the desire to ignore it and focus on the immediate tasks of reconstruction. The Allies' politics of reconstruction contributed here to the popular engagement – or lack thereof – with the immediate crimes of the Second World War and the Holocaust.

One aspect of reconstruction involved the creation of German polities out of the four Allies' zones of occupation. While the British, French and US zones would merge into the Federal Republic of Germany (FRG, or West Germany), the Soviet occupation zone became the German Democratic Republic (GDR, or East Germany). The very logic of the zones of occupation was born out of the desire to never again allow Germany to rise again and commit comparable crimes. For this goal, any new German polity would have to be 'de-Nazified' in the process of regaining independence. As Arendt commented in that same report from 1950, however, there was no good way to devise an effective system to uproot Nazism from German society.

To deal with the elite of the Nazi party and administration, the Allies turned to the courts. They instituted the Military International Tribunal that prosecuted twenty-one surviving important Nazi leaders and functionaries. These so-called Nuremberg Trials relied on a redrafted charter of legislation to include a new definition of Crimes against Humanity to face the gravity of the crimes of the Holocaust.[22] These trials were devised to demonstrate the responsibility of the German leadership for the war and particularly the crime of genocide. The latter

---

[19] Arendt, 'The Aftermath of Nazi Rule from Germany'.

[20] Stunde Null (or Zero Hour) refers to the political discourse that saw the liberation of Germany from its own Nazi regime as the beginning of a new German political trajectory, mostly popularised through Roberto Rossellini's 1948 film *Deutschland im Jahre Null*, see also Hobuß, 'Mythos "Stunde Null"', pp. 32–44.

[21] See, for example, the previously persecuted SPD deputy Paul Löbe's comment on the 'double flagellation' of the German people (Verhandlungen des Deutschen Bundestages, 1. Wahlperiode, 1. Sitzung, 7 September 1949, Stenographische Berichte, vol. 1, p. 2), or how the CDU politician Theodor Steltzer called the 'entire German people' to be declared victims of National Socialism (Reichel, *Vergangenheitsbewältigung in Deutschland*, p. 68).

[22] Bass, *Stay the Hand of Vengeance*.

was also a new definition, articulated by the legal scholar Rafael Lemkin following the seemingly unprecedented scale of the Holocaust's atrocities. Yet the very scope of the crime of genocide, which required mass participation on all levels beyond the leadership, made trials of the leadership insufficient for any social 'denazification'. The latter would have required dealing not only with individuals who perpetrated crimes but also with those who benefitted from them silently and supported the ideology that enabled them.

Denazification therefore needed to address the moral responsibility of German population to mass atrocities. In the immediate aftermath of liberation, Allied occupying forces that liberated concentration camps on German soil tried to confront ordinary people with the scale of these crimes, whether through forcing local population to bury bodies left in the camps or through erecting roadside signs with images of emaciated victims and the inscription 'These shameful atrocities: your guilt!'.[23] As Arendt noted, however, this 'finger pointing' mainly led to popular resentment at the occupiers' desire for 'revenge' rather than any introspection about collective guilt, or indeed moral indignation at the crimes these signs exposed.

Similarly, the Allies' plans for systemic denazification faced a contradiction from their very inception. On the one hand, occupation administrations needed to ascertain individuals' level of involvement with the National Socialist regime and ideology. On the other hand, however, they were confronted with the challenge of rebuilding functioning systems of governance and economy. The skilled workforce that was needed for these activities had operated mostly under the twelve years of Nazi dictatorship, where a requirement for work had been membership in the National Socialist Workers' Party (NSDAP).[24] As a result, the system of mass interviews designed to screen the population and categorise them based on their level of ideological complicity did not amount to confronting ordinary Germans with the meaning of crimes committed by the many degrees of their participation. Most people approached denazification committees as hurdles imposed by occupiers to be overcome so that they could move on with their lives. Arendt notes how people treated the certificate required for integration into the workforce as a 'Persilschein', or laundry certificate, that washed its holder of the stain of Nazi association and allowed them to bury the immediate past behind them.[25] The systems devised by the occupying forces faced the barriers of local intransigence and resentment at their imposition from the outside. If Germany later emerged as a laboratory for the politics of auto-critical memory, the immediate transition into the post-war era did not provide

---

[23] Arendt, 'The Aftermath of Nazi Rule from Germany', p. 344.

[24] Reichel, *Vergangenheitsbewältigung in Deutschland*, pp. 30–42.

[25] Arendt, 'The Aftermath of Nazi Rule from Germany', p. 344.

many signs for this development. These early days presented a conflict that would later be described by theorists of transitional justice as a paucity of 'domestic norm adopters', or Germans who wanted to deal with the Nazi past for their own sake rather than just to appease Allies.[26] To address questions of guilt and responsibility, German actors needed to establish a political rationale that tied these to ways of reinventing German society after the total defeat in the World War.

One exception to German popular and intellectual unwillingness to address immediate past was Hannah Arendt's friend and fellow philosopher Karl Jaspers. Unlike many German intellectuals – most notably Arendt's former lover Martin Heidegger – who aligned with and even supported the Nazi regime or who – like Arendt herself – left Germany, Jaspers spent the dictatorship years in Heidelberg, banned from publishing and awaiting deportation with his Jewish wife. After the 'liberation'[27] of Germany, Jaspers regained his university position and addressed students in a bombed lecture hall in Heidelberg for a lecture that would quickly be published as *The Question of German Guilt*.[28] Addressing the necessity to come to terms with Germany's place after its 'total' defeat, Jaspers suggested that a reckoning with guilt was not necessary because of the winners' demands, but to 'learn to talk with one another', to get 'spiritual bearings' and find 'common ground' in a society that had emerged out of a twelve-year dictatorship that had poisoned people's bearing of reality and interpersonal relations.[29] Jaspers then followed with definitions of guilt according to different types and its relevance to different sense of German individuals and collective – from the individual 'Criminal Guilt' to a 'Political Guilt' that affects political subjects through responsibility (Haftung), 'Moral Guilt' and lastly a 'Metaphysical Guilt' that affects all for simply having been present in a place where unspeakable crimes happened. Jaspers devised his 'methodological' analysis of guilt to address all levels of German society and counter any individual 'excuses' to avoid engagement with the question of guilt. While introducing categories of guilt that affected all, the philosopher insisted that guilt could not be collective in nature. He posited that every person needed to engage with guilt individually for the sake of future 'purification' that would enable Germans to overcome Nazi rule.[30]

---

[26] See Subotić, *Hijacked Justice*, pp. 33–36 and Olsen, Payne and Reiter, 'Demand for Justice: Domestic Support for Transitional Justice Mechanisms'.

[27] Many debates in Germany engaged with characterisation of the end of Nazi rule as 'liberation' or otherwise defeat and occupation. See, for example, Winkler, *Der lange Weg nach Westen*.

[28] Jaspers, *Die Schuldfrage*.   [29] Jaspers, *Die Schuldfrage*, p. 17.

[30] Jaspers, *Die Schuldfrage*, p. 91.

Jaspers did not write a political manual for 'coming to terms' with the immediate past, but delivered a philosophical manifesto that aimed at a future 'healing' of society. While he began his reflection on guilt from the desire to 'cleanse' German society, he did not do it from an abstract-moral perspective, nor did he perceive German society as a uniform collective of perpetrators. He articulated his categories of guilt to demonstrate that Germans needed to face their defeat – and their responsibility for it – if they wanted to rebuild a polity from the victory of the Allies. Jaspers' approach was an 'autocritical' one on the level of the individual (when speaking of guilt) and on the level of the political collective (when speaking of 'accountability' or 'responsibility').

In the same vein, the most important character of Jaspers' call for introspection was his focus on perpetrators rather than victims. For all later talk about German memory culture as a model for 'reconciliation', it is important to remember it emerged as an inter-German (and particularly West German) conversation that did not involve Jews, who often were absent from inter-German conversations. Post-war West Germany housed only a few surviving Jews, and these rarely sought to remain in the 'land of the perpetrators', let alone think of 'reconciliation'.[31] The earliest engagement with the question of 'Wiedergutmachung', or reparations to Jewish victims, did not occur as an inter-German debate, but on the state level. The Adenauer government signed the Luxemburg Agreement with David Ben Gurion's Israeli government and the Jewish Claims Conference with US support in 1952 despite popular resistance on the street and in the Bundestag.[32] For Jaspers, finding a way to move on then became a 'German' question that needed to be embraced by Germans themselves.

For all of Jaspers' engagement with the best way to face German guilt, he did not speak of memory. Jaspers' question of guilt addressed the connection between people's actions and the reshaping of a German polity in a period in which these actions were not yet confined to a time that was clearly past. As the Federal Republic regained its independence in the 1950s, perpetrators with different levels of involvement were inevitably integrated into society and state mechanisms. Here, the government and the public often avoided any large-scale political engagement with the legacies of crimes in the name of 'moving on' and ensuring peace though prosperity and the West German 'economic miracle'.[33] The past

---

[31] Brenner, *Nach dem Holocaust*.

[32] On the process of reparations, the debate in West Germany and the negotiations between the Adenauer government, the Israeli government and the Jewish Claims Conference, see Goldmann, *Mein Leben als deutscher Jude*, pp. 361–78, but especially Herbst and Goschler (eds.), *Wiedergutmachung in der Bundesrepublik Deutschland*.

[33] On the 'Economic Miracle, see Winkler, *Der lange Weg nach Westen*, but also Lindlar, *Das mißverstandene Wirtschaftswunder*.

was therefore something that needed to be overcome, rather than revisited. Two decades later, when the so-called 1968 generation initiated ever louder debates about their parents' crimes, they did so also for the sake of 'moving on', just with a different interpretation of what it meant.

1.2 The Road to 1968 and the Institutionalisation of Memory

While the 1950s did not showcase any large-scale memory debates in the Federal Republic, towards the end of the decade different intellectuals began claiming German society needed to face its 'past' in order to move on. One of the most influential of these interventions, which became a key moment in the gestation of the term 'Vergangenheitsbewältigung', was Theodor Adorno's publication of his lecture *Was bedeutet: Aufarbeitung der Vergangenheit* (often translated as 'The Meaning of Working through the Past') in 1959. Adorno addressed the 'processing' of the past in a period of political calm. This occurred just after the big controversies about the reinsertion of people 'burdened' with NS affiliations, but before the Eichmann Trial and other events brought back the NS past to the fore.[34] The Economic Miracle was in full swing, and rising prosperity only strengthened the general tendency to look away from the past.

Adorno, a voice of German moral introspection whose most well-known quote was about the barbarism of 'writing poetry after Auschwitz',[35] focused his intervention on the fragility of the newly established West German democracy. Fresh and lacking in traditional foundation, the philosopher claimed, democracy was in danger without a concerted effort to self-critically work through the past. Adorno did not yet foresee the politicisation of memory. For him, working through the past was the work of educators and psychologists, who needed to root out the moral foundations of Nazism in the psyche of the generation of perpetrators and their children, who would be exposed to these at home. Moreover, the philosopher contrasted the psychologised and individual 'moral dealing with the past' with a material, or 'objective' solution, which for him could only emerge through the demise of capitalism and the National Socialist material base. It is therefore noteworthy that autocritical introspection for Adorno was detached from what he considered as the 'political'. His moral stance became increasingly influential in the years leading to the 1968 student

---

[34] In 1961, the Israeli government located Adolf Eichmann, one of the architects of the 'Final Solution', in Argentina, kidnapped him and brought him to stand trial for crimes against humanity in Jerusalem. The trial became an international event through media coverage, not least through Hannah Arendt's book about it. See Arendt, *Eichmann in Jerusalem*.

[35] See Adorno, 'Kulturkritik und Gesellschaft', the text was written in 1949 and has often been misquoted as a moral rejection of art production after the Holocaust.

protests, in which ideas about working through the past crystallised into a new generational identity.

Adorno's intervention attracted growing visibility through the march of current events. These included the attack on Cologne's newly opened synagogue on Christmas Eve of 1959 by members of the Nazi grouping *Deutsche Reichspartei* (German Reich Party, DRP). The attack prompted the then Chancellor Konrad Adenauer to react directly to the event a few days later in his speech at the commemoration of the liberation of the concentration camp Bergen Belsen with a call to assure that National Socialist crimes could never be repeated.[36] The televised trial of Adolf Eichmann in Jerusalem in 1961[37] and then the Auschwitz Trials in Frankfurt between 1963 and 1965[38] returned Nazi crimes and perpetrators to the headlines. Much has been written about how the staging of the Eichmann Trial through the testimonies of survivors initiated what Annette Wieviorka named the 'era of the witness' with a specific focus on victims' testimonies.[39] Yet it also confronted the world – and not least German society – with what Hannah Arendt defined the 'banality of evil'[40]: the very ordinary face of the technocratic perpetrator. What Adorno called on his fellow Germans to 'process', and the things that would occupy German memory over the next few decades, did not focus on the victims and their stories. Instead, it involved facing the ubiquity of legacies of ordinary perpetrators in Germany. Interest in the identities and ubiquity of perpetrators trickled down to popular culture as well. One example was Günther Grass' first book *Die Blechtrommel* (The Tin Drum) from 1959, which portrayed German history as that of petty passivity and collaboration. Simultaneously, the 1960s also saw the publication of works like Rolf Hochhuth's play *Der Stellvertreter* (The Deputy, 1963) on the Catholic Church's relationship with National Socialism, or Peter Weiss' play *Die Ermittlung. Oratorium in elf Gesängen* (The Investigation, 1965) about the Auschwitz Processes. These works reflected growing public attention to the broad German involvement in the Nazi machine and challenged narratives that portrayed the majority population as 'following orders', unaware of crimes committed in their name.

---

[36] See Adenauer, 'Im deutschen Volk hat der Nationalsozialismus keine Wurzel', p. 89.

[37] See Arendt, *Eichmann in Jerusalem*.

[38] The Auschwitz Trials in Frankfurt were the most important and visible trials of twenty-two Nazi criminals in West Germany and took place between 1963 and 1965. For the trial's documentation see Fritz Bauer Institut and Staatliches Museum Auschwitz-Birkenau (eds.), *Der Auschwitz-Prozess*.

[39] Wieviorka coined the term to refer to the centrality of survivors and witness accounts in making sense of history. See Wieviorka, *L'Ère du témoin*.

[40] Arendt's coining of the 'banality of evil' emerged from her coverage of the Eichmann Trial, in which she described the ordinariness of Nazi perpetrators, and particularly of Eichmann, in committing 'evil' act. See Arendt, *Eichmann in Jerusalem*.

These strands of 'facing the past' crystallised into a coherent identity through the 1968 student movement. Just as in other European countries, whether France, Italy or even Denmark, the '1968 movement' was not always a coherent movement, but emerged from growing student activism that reacted to issues as diverse as conservative government structures (in the case of West Germany the Grand Coalition that came to power in 1966 after the long Adenauer era), the Vietnam War, grievances with university hierarchies and a sense of generational change and resentment to the 'old guard'. The latter, with such popular slogans like 'trust no-one over 30', produced a cohesive mythology even after the movements that encapsulated the 1968 moment had dissipated.[41] Disparate student mobilisations gave birth to a mythology of the '1968 generation' that had 'confronted their parents' about their participation in Nazi crimes.[42]

Nonetheless, the coherence of the '1968 generation' was a retrospective projection rather than reality on the ground. Different historians like Norbert Frei, Kurt Sontheimer and Hermann Lübbe all spent the better part of the 2000s discussing the actual engagement of the student movement with the idea of *Vergangenheitsbewältigung*, and often reached the conclusion that this had been often largely exaggerated.[43] Much student engagement with the 'past' indeed amounted to mere discursive strategies. These included the use of the epithet 'fascist' to attack their adversaries – of any political colours – in the contemporary Federal Republic rather than remembering the past. One such example was the comparison of the 1968 Grand Coalition's Emergency Act to a 'second 1933' or the constant comparison of the Conservative party the Christian Democratic Union (CDU) to National Socialist bodies.[44]

Nonetheless, these discursive strategies reflected two elements that were key in the later understanding of what German memory was. The first was considering the rejection of fascism as a new – and in this case generational – identity of the German left. The second was the acknowledgement of the actual continuities of National Socialist world views in West German society. Here, student engagement also addressed the presence of former Nazi members in German institutions, most visibly through debates about Kurt Georg Kiesinger,

---

[41] Schildt, *Rebellion und Reform*. On the continuities between 1968 and left-wing terrorism of the 1970s, see Kraushaar(ed.), *Die RAF und der linke Terrorismus*.

[42] See Kraushaar, *1968 als Mythos, Chiffre und Zäsur*.

[43] See, for example, Lübbe, *Die Aufdringlichkeit der Geschichte*, Sontheimer, 'Gegen den Mythos von 1968'.

[44] Different brochures constantly compared the Grand Coalition with the Nazi regimes, see, for example, 'Grosse [sic!] Koalition und Notstandsgesetze oder: Wie man die Demokratie begräbt und das Volk verschaukelt', Universitätsarchiv Heidelberg SDS FB 1.1 1967–1969, but also Klimke and Mausbach, 'Auf der äußeren Linie der Befreiungskriege', p. 24.

the Grand Coalition chancellor and the only ever former member of the National Socialist Workers' Party to have been elected chancellor in West Germany. Much of the symbolism of the 1968 student movement's addressing the past can be perceived through the slapping of Kiesinger by the journalist Beate Klarsfeld (who was not a member of the '68 student movement) at the CDU party conference in Berlin in 1967. Klarsfeld later described her action as a desire to show the world that 'a part of German society [. . .]rebels against the fact that a Nazi now stands at the helm of the Federal Government'.[45] For Klarsfeld, just as for others of the '68 generation, confronting the past made sense as a way to prove – often to other nations – that young Germans who had not experienced the war personally had indeed moved away from the crimes of their parents' generation. This element was particularly important in the motivation to 'move on' in moral debates about coming to terms with the past, as a way to regain standing as equals in post-war Europe.

If '68ers addressed the past as a matter of identity, their actions did not amount to an institutional 'memory' of it. Many '68ers demonstrated a contradiction between open protest against their parents' generation and a difficulty to articulate what confronting the past would mean to them. Here, many activists returned to Adorno's focus on psychology as a way to address the past, often relying on a new popular text by the Freudian psychoanalysts Margarete and Alexander Mitscherlich, *Die Unfähigkeit zu trauern* (The Inability to Mourn, 1967).[46] For the Mitscherlichs, the only way to move on required confronting the memories of the past that had been transmitted from the parents' generation. However, the psychologisation of the process did not facilitate calls for any political process that would enable this 'dealing with the past'. A few years later, however, a spontaneous gesture by the chancellor Willy Brandt in Warsaw became the symbol of an institutional adoption of individual introspection of the past.

Brandt, a Social Democrat who had been foreign minister under the Grand Coalition (1966–9) and the then chancellor (1969–74), became a symbol of 'new politics' with a call for 'daring more democracy'.[47] This daring, for Brandt, included articulating politics through confrontation with the Nazi past, which stood in stark contrast with Adenauer's policy of minimal engagement with the Nazi past to avoid challenges to West Germany's fragile democracy.[48] Brandt's

---

[45] See, for example, Interview with Beate Klarsfeld, Frankfurter Rundschau, 29 June 2006, in which she referred to the slapping. For contextualisation, see Gassert, 'Die Klarsfeld-Ohrefeige'.

[46] See Mitscherlich and Margarete, *Die Unfähigkeit zu trauern*.

[47] See Herf, *Divided Memory*, pp. 344–45.

[48] Adenauer avoided German responsibility in German debates, yet addressed these in his engagement with international actors, most notably in negotiations with Jewish organisations and Israeli officials. As in a speech in 1951, he defined his politics as that of 'Wiedergutmachung', or

signature *Ostpolitik*, rapprochement with Eastern Europe, relied on his understanding of the need to fight mistrust of Germany fuelled by its politics of silence.
In his 1968 book, he acknowledged: 'I do not ever forget that it was Hitler's
"Greater Germany" above all that brought so much unspeakable suffering to
Eastern Europe'.[49] In December 1970, as a part of the thaw between Bonn and its
eastern neighbours, Brandt visited Warsaw to sign a contract that initiated the
'normalisation' of relations between Poland and the Federal Republic. On a visit
to the memorial of the Warsaw Ghetto Uprising, in front of many cameras
present, Brandt suddenly went on his knees and lowered his head in silence.
The spontaneous and emotional gesture, which was captured on cameras and
then circulated around the world, soon became a symbol of German contrition
and willingness to face the past. The kneeling's sense of authentic emotion in
front of a memorial coupled with Brandt's status as chancellor created an
image that applied the myth of '68ers' 'facing the past' with the institution of
the Federal Republic. The kneeling became a 'memory site', or a moment that
fostered a new West German identity as a willingness to lower one's head to
acknowledge the weight of the past. For the creation of this memorial identity,
the actual immediate reactions to the gesture mattered less. Brandt's gesture
was not met with unanimous approval back home at the time, nor did it
impress all the Polish hosts, who would have preferred a show of emotion in
front of a more national site rather than a Jewish one.[50] What did matter was
the symbol of a German chancellor adopting the emotional charge of debates
that had hitherto taken place on different levels, but never gained the state's
stamp of approval.

The aftermath of Brandt's kneeling provided the context for the model of
autocritical memory, which cemented over the two subsequent decades. It was
most visible in the speech of the West German President, Richard von
Weizsäker, on 8 May 1985, which commemorated the fortieth anniversary of
the 'liberation' of Germany from its own Nazi rule.[51] The underlying rationale
for the concept coalesced out of debates about the best way to establish
a democratic (West) Germany that 'moved on' from the burdens of Nazi
association. The importance of 'memory' emerged in the case of generations
of Germans who, to use Karl Jaspers' definition, bore no 'criminal guilt' for
having perpetrated crimes, but needed to come to terms with the 'political guilt',
or the accountability associated with belonging to the political entity in whose

---

reparations, see Adenauer, Konrad, speech on 27 September 1951, www.konrad-adenauer.de/
seite/27-september-1951/ (last accessed 23 February 2023).
[49] Brandt, *Friedenspolitik in Europa*, p. 148.   [50] Fink and Schaefer, *Ostpolitik, 1969–1974*.
[51] Von Weizsäker, *Rede zur Gedenkveranstaltung im Plenarsaal des Deutschen Bundestages zum
40.*

name these crimes had been committed. Acknowledging the specificity of German crimes became a cornerstone of the articulation of a new West German identity that needed to articulate a new German democratic culture. The importance of the concept *Vergangenheitsbewältigung* to West German self-perception then became even more pronounced in the *Historikerstreit*, or historians' dispute, in 1986–9. The dispute saw right-wing and left-wing intellectuals appear on television and in newspapers to debate the 'singularity' of both the crimes of the Holocaust and German history, and mostly how the past *should* impact German national identity.[52] It was here that the '68er philosopher Jürgen Habermas, while condemning right-wing historians' 'revisionist' tendencies, lambasted the very idea of German pride after the crimes of the Second World War. New German patriotism, he suggested, should come from an identity anchored in European cooperation and a democratic German constitution.[53] Habermas' call for 'constitutional patriotism' echoed the idea that any kind of German identity needed to first and foremost be based on self-criticism facing remembrance of the very German character of Nazi crimes. The success of equating 'dealing with the past' with a new German national identity became all too visible thirty years later, as journalists and politicians began discussing jokingly Germany's status as a 'world champion in dealing with the past' in the run-up to the European Football Championship in 2012.[54] This sense of irony reflected the understanding that German identity in the 2000s had become closely entwined with the concept of remembering its own dark past, so much so that 'dealing with the past' had morphed into a new kind of national pride.

Simultaneously, as autocritical memory had become a component of national identity in Germany, it remained mostly a subject of inner-German conversations rather than a dialogue with descendants of victims. One of the motivations of addressing Germany's dark past was often related to a German desire to 'normalise' the country's image internationally, as German investment in massive programmes of exchanges with France, Poland and Israel suggest.[55] Jewish or Polish actors, however, were mostly absent from debates in Germany, which remained focused on Karl Jaspers' opening premise in *The Question of Guilt*: that Germans needed to relearn 'how to speak with one another'.[56] In this vein, the adoption of a 'memory culture' in Germany opened up conversations about

---

[52] For texts of the Historikerstreit, see Augstein and Bracher (eds.), *Historikerstreit*.

[53] Habermas, 'Eine Art Schadensabwicklung', also in Augstein and Bracher, *Historikerstreit*, pp. 62–68.

[54] See, for example, the radio show 'Weltmeister in Vergangenheitsbewältigung', in *Deutschlandfunk Kultur*, 07 February 2012.

[55] Gardner Feldman, 'The Principle and Practice of "Reconciliation" in German Foreign Policy', pp. 333–56.

[56] Jaspers, *Die Schuldfrage*, p. 13.

the kind of democracy Germans wanted to create (and sustain). The guidelines of memory in Germany became ever more visible in the construction of museums and memorials, whether the Documentation Centre at the Nazi Party Rally Grounds in Nurnberg (2001) or the Holocaust Memorial in Berlin (2005). School curricula became ever more focused on the National Socialist past and the question of German responsibility – including to the State of Israel – in the present. In the third generation, beginning in the 1990s, a number of young Germans interrogated their family history and the transmission of stories about grandparents' Nazi past, most notable through the successful book *Opa war kein Nazi* (Grandfather was not a Nazi, 2002).[57] These remained conversations post-war Germans had with themselves in a country that was no longer home to its pre-war Jewish community.

The so-called German model relied on a set of contradictions. For outside observers, Germany's culture of autocritical memory made sense in the context of the country's transformation: after twelve years of Nazi rule and a war of annihilation, Germans unexpectedly refocused their energy on rebuilding what seemed to be a peaceful polity. The prosperity of the Federal Republic, which was dependent on the European project and international export, relied on an image of a repentant West German state where governments 'wrote the checks' for others. Many would later come to suggest that it was Germany's memory culture that enabled reconstruction, prosperity and re-integration in Europe. However, it was the prosperity that paved the way for the emergence of a German memory culture in the second and third generations after the war. While the establishment of autocritical memory in Germany became a marker of successful addressing of responsibility in public and in the political sphere, the very inner-German character of these debates meant that it had never been a tool for fighting racism, achieving reconciliation or even fostering conversations with descendants of victims.

1.3 A Duty to Remember: Autocritical Memory in France

While the 'German Model' is often used as reference for successful 'dealing with the past', another autocritical model of remembering the Holocaust developed in France in parallel, and often through observation of developments across the River Rhein in Germany. Just as in Germany, the French model of the *'Devoir de mémoire'* (Duty to remember) had become a political rationale for state actors. Simultaneously, it emerged from demands of victims and their descendants rather than as a pure Franco-French debate.

---

[57] Moller, Tschuggnall and Welzer, *'Opa war kein Nazi'*.

French and West German societies were not confronted with the exact same challenge when facing the memory of the Second World War. Germans needed to face Germany's responsibility for the war; French society needed to face the legacies of occupation. The main fault line that divided society was the distinction between categories of 'resistance' and 'collaboration' with German occupiers and the collaborationist Vichy regime.[58] In the immediate post-war period, purges of collaborators made way for amnesty laws that reintegrated collaborationists into society and the Gaullist government's formulation of what the historian Henry Rousso called the 'resistentialist myth'.[59] To 'move on', rebuild and unite fractured society in the aftermath of the war, Gaullist governments crafted a narrative of a 'resisting France', which portrayed collaboration as inherently un-French.

As in Germany, however, the Gaullist compromise came under fire during the student and worker mobilisation of May 1968. Yet the specificities of the Second World War played a less prominent role in France than in Germany's intergenerational strife. Crimes of the parents' generation served as a way of framing conservative leaders or bosses, as in French student gatherings participants lambasted their adversaries as '*collabos*' (collaborators) and '*tortionnaires*' (torturers, alluding to the practice of torture in the Algerian War of Independence) interchangeably. Here, students marked a generational fault line in the same way as in Germany, but focused less on its historical specificity and far more on resentment to French conservative hierarchies. Historical references in the '68 movement were even less coherent than in Germany, as 'dealing with the past' remained lower on students' and workers' priorities than protesting de Gaulle as a representative of conservative hierarchies. Despite the president's authoritarian streak, de Gaulle was still the symbol of French external resistance and the man who negotiated the end of French presence in Algeria, and therefore not a coherent target for condemning Vichyite nostalgia.[60] With all its lack of cohesion and failure to topple de Gaulle, '68 nonetheless ushered cultural change in France, which enabled some public engagement with the Vichy past in the early 1970s. One trigger for this increased public attention was the publication of American historian Robert Paxton's book *Vichy France: Old Guard and New Order* (1972, translated into French in 1973), which claimed the collaboration was the fruit of French choice.[61] The so-called Paxtonian Revolution, which

---

[58] See, for example, Kedward, *Occupied France* and *The French Resistance and Its Legacy* and Jackson, *France: The Dark Years, 1940–1944*.

[59] Rousso, Le Syndrome de Vichy de 1944 à nos jours.

[60] On the contradictions of the sixty-eight student movements, see various contributions in Jackson, Milne and Williams (eds.), *May 1968: Rethinking France's Last Revolution*.

[61] Paxton, *Vichy France*, p. 51.

Henry Rousso later described as a phase of forced French introspection, followed the release of Marcel Ophuls' film *Le Chagrin et la pitié* (The Sorrow and the Pity, 1972). The documentary, which consisted in interviews with ordinary people, demonstrated the extent of voluntary collaboration. Both works shattered the image of a French society that was supposedly united by the spirit of resistance, or at least pushed to collaboration by lack of choice and fear of the consequences of refusal. Another element of novelty in the debates in 1973 was the increasing focus on the persecution of Jews as one main aspect of collaboration, particularly one that transcended some of the grey zones between collaboration and resistance.

The fate of Jews in France had not been central to most debates about the war in the immediate post-war years. Annette Wieviorka posited that for the left, the story of Jewish deportees had been subsumed under the 'greater' overarching story of Communist and resistant deportees.[62] Simultaneously, the resistentialist myth did not leave much space to discuss the particularity of the German persecution of Jews – compared to other French citizens – or the responsibility of French individuals, organisations (such as the police) and the Vichy regime for the deportation of Jews. Some Jewish actors, like the group *Amicale des anciens déportés Juifs de France* (The Friends of Former French Jewish Deportees, AADFJ), demanded their stories be recognised by French politicians, while France's main representative Jewish organisations created their own memory routines. The most notable of these was the annual commemoration of the Vél D'hiv Roundup (or the Winter Velodrome Roundup), when French police officers had rounded up around 13,000 Parisian Jews to be sent to death on 16 July 1942.[63] Nonetheless, broader interest in Jewish victims first crystallised in the 1960s, after the witness testimonies of the Eichmann Trial in 1961 and later Jewish resentment towards what they perceived as a betrayal of the French state due to its reaction to the Six Day War between Israel and the Arab States in 1967.[64] By the thirtieth commemoration of the Vél d'Hiv Roundup in 1972, the very specific targeting of Jews by French institutions during the war had become a special component of debates about collaboration.

The most important actors in the emergence of a public memory of the Holocaust in France were Jewish movements, and a growing number of memory associations, which became increasingly active during the 1970s. These activists embraced the voices of witnesses and addressed the need to remember the Holocaust, but with very specific goals in the present day. They linked the

---

[62] Wieviorka, *Déportation et génocide*.

[63] Ledoux, 'Silence et oubli de la mémoire de la Shoah: une « illusion » historiographique?', pp. 76–93 and Rousso, *Le Syndrome de Vichy de 1944 à nos jours*.

[64] Wolf, *Harnessing the Holocaust*.

rise of Holocaust denial in the present with the impunity of Vichy criminals, who could not be brought to trial because of amnesty laws from the 1950s. Remembering the specific fate of Jewish victims, then, required a special focus on the French state's responsibility in the persecution of its own Jewish citizens, whether by the Vichy state or institutions like the Paris police that operated under German occupation. Jewish activists thus demanded the French state to take their voice into account as French citizens.

One of the most visible Jewish militants for the memory of the Holocaust was the lawyer Serge Klarsfeld, who took the public stage together with his German wife Beate Klarsfeld, who was remembered in Germany for slapping the President Kiesinger. The couple published the list of Jewish deportees to Auschwitz in 1978 under the title *Mémorial de la déportation des Juifs de France*, fought for compensation for Jewish survivors through the association *Fils et filles des déportés juifs de France* (Sons and Daughters of French Jewish Deportees, founded in 1979) and were key actors in new attempts to bring Vichy officials to justice. In 1983, the Klarsfelds located the German war criminal Klaus Barbie in Bolivia and played a key part in his extradition and then trial in France in 1987, when he was found guilty of Crimes against humanity.[65] These different actions reflected the ways Jewish actors interpreted memorial justice in the 1970s, which, for them, needed to be delivered by the state.

In the 1980s, the French dimension of the Shoah[66] became increasingly visible in mainstream French cultural production with the publication of historical works, whether the French translation of Raul Hillberg's work or Henry Rousso's *The Vichy Syndrome* (1984) and feature films, such as Louis Malle's autobiographical *Au Revoir les Enfants* (1987). Nonetheless, even with the rise of François Mitterrand's left-wing governments, the state did not answer Jewish calls to acknowledge the republic's responsibility for collaboration and deportation of French Jews. For President Mitterrand, as he memorably stated in a television interview in 1992 when asked about his position on a demand issued by the group *Comité Vel d'Hiv 42*, 'one should not ask for accountability from the republic', as the republic was not responsible for any actions of the Vichy government.[67] In this period, however, Jewish actors began formulating demands for memorial accountability by the state through the vocabulary of '*Devoir de mémoire*', or Duty

---

[65] Ledoux, 'Des « origines » du « devoir de mémoire » aux sources de la mémoire de la Shoah: historiciser la mémoire de son oubli'.

[66] The Hebrew name for the Holocaust, which began being used in France after Claude Lanzmann's 1979 groundbreaking documentary of testimonies with that same name.

[67] François Mitterrand in interview with Gérard Carreyou, *Journal de 13h*, TF1, 14 July 1992.

to remember. At first, that 'Duty to remember' could just as well be interpreted as the state's Duty to remember those who had given their lives for the state, as was the case in speeches of Ministers of Veterans in the 1980s.[68] As of the early 1990s, however, Jewish organisations and politicians began using the formula to address the state's obligation to remember its own victims, or in this case Jews who had been rounded up by French policemen and deported through the actions of French collaborators. In 1995, the then newly elected president Jacques Chirac earned the nickname of the 'Devoir de Mémoire President',[69] as he stated the Duty to remember as a republican rationale as he attended the Vél d'Hiv commemoration and recognised the French state's responsibility for collaborating with the 'occupant's criminal folly'.[70]

In Chirac's speech, which has since become one of the most quoted speeches of the French Fifth Republic, the French head of state articulated a concept of autocritical memory. Unlike the German model, which relied much more on social introspection and recognition of crimes, in France the state played an active role in the 'Duty to remember'. The state's duty to actively remember its own crimes would then become a permanent fixture of French politics (see Section 3), as it informed an increased political engagement with memory. 'Remembering' the crimes – and thus the responsibility – of the French state became a part of school curricula, political debates and speeches and other memorial actions such as the construction of physical memorials in France. Another difference to the German model that has been mentioned previously was the active role of French Jews in the articulation of this memorial model. Here victims and their descendants were key players in the creation of a memory discourse. Yet, for the French intellectuals and activists who participated in debates about the need to acknowledge the crimes of the French state, memory – and with it the focus on the French state's responsibility – was a way to address their belonging as French citizens who had been failed by the state. Jewish actors articulated their demands to the state through the vocabulary of citizenship and duty rather than that of 'reconciliation', which assumed a psychological process. Jewish actors participated in the creation of an autocritical memory model, in which confronting the crimes of the past for the sake of present-day state responsibility mattered more than foregrounding victims' voices in a moral debate.

---

[68] Ledoux, *Le Devoir de mémoire*.

[69] Lotem, *The Memory of Colonialism in Britain and France*, p. 161.

[70] Chirac, *Allocution du Président de la République prononcée lors des cérémonies commémorant la grande rafle des 16 et 17 juillet 1942*.

1.4 Conclusion: Autocritical Memory and Holocaust Remembrance in the 2000s

Over the second half of the twentieth century, two models of autocritical memory developed in parallel in West Germany and France. In France in particular, German actors like the student activist Daniel Cohn Bandit and the journalist Beate Klarsfeld participated in the creation of this narrative through borrowing from West German developments. In both cases, changing public debates, intellectual and cultural production, activist mobilisation and political reactions coalesced into a new memory rationale, in which polities addressed their own crimes. In both cases, the establishment of such models, if one can call them so, required a mix of lively public interest and state adoption of the rationale of auto criticism. In both cases, moreover, the acceptance of the need to engage in such autocritical remembrance only materialised with a generational shift. A second generation that had not been personally involved in the war had taken the reins of power and was able to engage with memory politics without any elements of personal responsibility or guilt. Autocritical memory thus offered a way to re-imagine political identities in either polity through focus on self-reflection. Nonetheless, in neither case did the emergence of autocritical memory truly focus on 'reconciliation' between victims and perpetrators. This is particularly noteworthy in the German case, where the autocritical nature of West German memory politics never emerged through dialogue with victims and their descendants, but opened up new avenues of thinking about German identities in a society with practically no Jews left.

These two models of autocritical remembrance focused on the role of memory in national debates, structures and identities, at a time when Holocaust memory worldwide was becoming increasingly defined by appeals to universality.[71] For example, between 1995 and 2005, the EU Parliament and the UN's General Assembly both accepted resolutions that reiterated the importance of Holocaust commemoration and education to use lessons from the Second World War for the sake of 'liberties and human values'[72] and to 'help prevent future genocides'.[73] In popular culture, films like *Schindler's List* and *La Vita è bella* became international successes that reflected how the Holocaust became a subject of globalised audiences. The emergence of visible Holocaust museums in places like Washington, DC, in the US, Curritiba in

---

[71] Baer and Sznaider, *Memory and Forgetting in the Post-Holocaust Era*, pp. 9–15.

[72] European Parliament Resolution of 27 April 1995 on racism, xenophobia and anti-Semitism (OJ C 126, 22 May 1995).

[73] United Nations, Security Council, 'The Rule of Law and Transnational Justice in Conflict and Post-Conflict Societies. Report of the Secretary General'. S/2004/616, 23 August 2004.

Brazil, Montreal in Canada or Hong Kong, where the Holocaust had not taken place, reflected a growing appeal of the 'remembering' the Holocaust with a universalist message of 'never again'.

Simultaneously, national debates in Germany and France revolved around the polities of former perpetrators. Emerging globalising paradigms of Holocaust memory, meanwhile, stressed the importance of focusing on the voices of victims, rather than the questions of the perpetrators' motives, strategies and methods. This points out to a contradiction in the examination of autocritical memory. While the so-called German model of introspection quickly became hailed as a success story and formed the base of devising institutional ways of 'dealing with the past', that very model emerged from very specific German conditions and as such did not raise any of the universal issues it was used to address. Section 2 therefore examines the development of institutionalised memory politics that sought to build on that 'German model' in contexts of democratisation. Section 3 examines the expansion of memory politics to address colonial crimes alongside the Holocaust, and in so doing to mobilise the German model to try and fight racism.

2 Autocritical Memory and Democratisation: Memory as a 'Model'

The 'End of History', and optimism of the 1990s,[74] supported many in the belief that conflicts can be overcome through models that had been tested following the Second World War. The 'third wave of democratisation'[75] strengthened Westernised impressions of advancing (liberal) democracies. As new polities transitioned into democracy, however, international organisations and observers began searching for ways to manage democratisation, not least in the aftermath of violent conflicts, such as the genocides in Rwanda and Bosnia and Herzegovina. This section explores the rise of memory as an international model of democratisation. International actors sought to create a transferrable model based on what they perceived as 'successes' of the German, the Argentinian and South African transformations. In so doing, they developed a list of 'best practice' actions that were supposed to be implemented in transitions into democracy, but which relied on ahistorical readings of the specificities of successful transitions (and simultaneously ignored the less successful elements

---

[74] The concept of the End of History became popularly identified with the sense of Western triumphalism over Communism after the end of the Cold War, based on Francis Fukuyama's book with the same name, see Fukuyama, *The End of History and the Last Man*.

[75] The 'third wave of democratisation' refers to the global democratic transformations from the 1970s – mainly in Latin America – to the shifts following the break up of the Soviet Union. See Diamond, 'Democracy's Third Wave Today'.

of each transition). The universalisation of a model that Lea David calls 'moral remembrance' became a powerful discursive tool, but also failed in achieving long-lasting transitions. The cases of Serbia and Poland, two democratic transitions in Central and Eastern Europe, illustrate how the development of memory politics into universalist 'victim-oriented' frames and away from the autocritical rationale failed to capture the specific elements that had made autocritical thinking so successful in the first place. In both cases, nationalist actors were able to hijack debates about memory and focus on victimhood rather than the meaning of history for descendants of perpetrators.

2.1 The Invention of Transitional Justice

Just as the memory of the Holocaust was becoming ever more globalised, international actors began appropriating memory into a model of 'transition' into democracy. This section follows the emergence of the concept of 'transitional justice' and its elevation into a toolkit for 'reconciliation' and 'healing'. Its gestation, however, also demonstrates its main weakness. Actors borrowed from different case studies that were historically specific and sought to create a 'best practice' model of memory that could be implemented anywhere at will. Through the ahistorical mixing and matching, they created a normatively appealing concept of memory, which remained detached from the realities and specificities of each society it was applied to.

In the 1990s, decision makers worldwide began paying attention to a new concept, or at least a newly articulated one. Between 1988 and the mid-1990s, transitional justice became fashionable, then institutional, in international governance networks, human rights groups and NGOs.[76] One of the components of this new concept became the importance of memory in post-conflict societies. It developed a model of what 'proper' remembrance of atrocities should look like.[77]

In 1988, the US-based Aspen Institute organised a conference in Wye, Maryland, entitled 'State Crimes: Punishment or Pardon' that united delegates from places as varied as the US, Argentina, Brazil, Uganda, the Philippines, or South Africa, to discuss the implications of measures devised to expose human rights abuses of previous regimes in transitions to democracy.[78] This became the first of four international conferences between 1988 and 1995 that articulated the concept of transitional justice. Each conference reflected the changing priorities of transnational justice activists, as the 1992 conference in Salzburg

---

[76] See Moyn, *The Last Utopia* and Subotić, *Hijacked Justice*, pp. 20–23.

[77] David, 'The Emergence of the "Dealing with the Past" Agenda', p. 6.

[78] Arthur, 'How "Transitions" Reshaped Human Rights'.

debated the Central and Eastern European cases after the collapse of the Iron Curtain and the 1994 conference in Cape Town discussed the South African case. The first conference, however, was dominated by the case of Argentina, which informed much of the early thinking on transitional justice and memory.

The Argentinian case foregrounded the role of 'coming to terms with the past' in legitimating a democratic regime that replaced a dictatorship. As the military Junta collapsed in 1983 following the Falklands War, the new democratically elected government led by Raul Alfonsín faced the necessity to legitimate itself and delegitimate the dictatorship.[79] It needed to create mechanisms to 'move on'; yet targeting of 'collaborators' would risk the new regime's stability. Unlike in Nurnberg and the process of denazification, the new government was not a foreign victor, but required popular support. It also relied on a judiciary that had not been purged since the Junta. It thus opted for limited prosecution of the latter's leaders, who were later pardoned, while initiating a public debate on their regime's crimes. The debate was saturated with references to Nazi crimes not only due to the use of concentration camps but also for the many parallels in ideology between the Junta and Nazi Germany.[80] However, one of the challenges facing Argentinian institutions was the old regime's methods of disposing of bodies, thus leaving no physical evidence or witnesses. To document the crimes and victims, the *desaparecidos* (the Disappeared), the most notable memorial action of the new regime, was the report *Nunca Más* (Never Again, published in 1983). The report's name established a link to Holocaust memory, while the body of the report contained many references and comparisons to the Holocaust and Nazi crimes. Methodologically, however, the report functioned as one of the first 'truth commissions' that denounced crimes rather than trying to find legal evidence. Using hundreds of individual testimonies to paint a picture of the Junta's state terror, the report prepared Argentinians for the eventual Junta trials. Like the Eichmann Trial two decades earlier, it established the importance of the witness for the paradigm of *verdad-memoria-justicia* (truth-memory-justice) that would be the hallmark of Argentinian 'coming to terms with the past'.[81]

The 1988 conference used the Argentinian example as a success story of transition from dictatorship into democracy, to provide evidence for regimes in neighbouring countries and beyond, including Brazil, Uruguay, Chile and the Philippines. It thus began a process of creating a model for 'transitions' into democracy in a period in which a growing number of international institutions perceived establishing democratic cultures worldwide as a shared political goal.

---

[79] Teitel, *Transitional Justice.*   [80] Finchelstein, *The Ideological Origins of the Dirty War.*

[81] Baer and Sznaider, *Memory and Forgetting in the Post-Holocaust Era*, pp. 31–32.

The people who formulated this model – who participated in the 1988 and further conferences and published what became the key texts on the subject – were a mixed group of political scientists like John Herz, Neil Kritz or Ruti Teitel; democracy activists and dissidents such as Adam Michnik, Joachin Gauck or José Zalaquett; and self-proclaimed 'social entrepreneurs' like Timothy Phillips.[82] The absence of historians was notable. Participants approached case studies without a sense of historical specificities, but rather through the search of 'best practice' models for universal action. Starting with the Argentinian and German examples, participants identified a set of measures that would come to characterise transitional justice: prosecutions, truth-telling, restitution and reparation.

Over the following years, the understanding of these 'measures' developed, as activists and academics rearticulated the purpose of 'transition' to address shifts in international attention to world events. While the first conference focused on fragile transitions into democracy following regime changes in South America, the 1992 Salzburg conference participants perceived transition as an inevitable tide of history. The fall of communism had ushered in triumphalism. One of the focuses of the conference was the German case, in which transition meant the GDR's incorporation into the Federal Republic. German participants, most of whom were West German except for the East German dissident Joachim Gauck, spoke about the necessity to face the oppressive nature of the Stasi and the GDR dictatorship. In 1994, the Cape Town conference focused on the South African case with attention to the role of truth commissions in the transition from Apartheid to democracy. The goal of 'reconciliation' was the rationale of public reckoning with the crimes of a former regime. This conference, however, took place just at a time when transitional justice, as the term would be defined after 1995 with the publication of the influential book by Neil Kritz,[83] shifted its focus onto the post-conflict (and post-genocide) cases of Rwanda and the Western Balkans. In the second half of the 1990s and the early 2000s, international organisations adopted the transitional justice model as ubiquitous guideline – and a moral imperative – to dealing with societies in the aftermath of conflicts.[84] The establishment of international criminal tribunals for those responsible for the perpetration of war crimes, as the ICTY in former Yugoslavia (1993), the ICTR in Rwanda (1994) and the International Criminal Court (ICC, 1998), was a further sign of the impact of the rationale of transitional justice on international actors.

---

[82] Mouralis, 'The Invention of "Transitional Justice" in the 1990s', pp. 83–100.

[83] Kritz, *Transitional Justice*.

[84] See Subotić, *Hijacked Justice*, p. 3; David, 'The Emergence of the "Dealing with the Past" Agenda', p. 8.

The defining principle of transitional justice was that 'moving on' and anchoring democratic principles in newly established democracies required facing the crimes of dictatorships. The conferences and the 1995 volume thus contrasted two European 'models'. On the one hand stood the Spanish model of 'pact of silence' following the Civil War, which did not bring the appeasement and the establishment of a stable democracy.[85] On the other was West Germany's *Vergangenheitsbewältigung*, which by the late 1980s seemed like a success story. The purpose of trials, truth commissions, commemorations and reparation measures was to promote social healing and thus reconciliation between perpetrators and victims. The lack of historicisation of the models from which political thinkers borrowed, however, created a set of moral expectations from a model that had never truly succeeded in the conditions of post-conflict transition. The kind of social reconciliation that the Argentinian – and later South African – models promoted was not only internal but also partial at best, while the German model provided no blueprint for reconciliation, as it remained focused on an internal German conversation.[86]

In fact, it is particularly in relation to the so-called German model that the contradictions of the systematisation of transitional justice measures became apparent. Firstly, in conversations about harnessing what was perceived as German successes, an idea of a 'German model' encompassed three very different transformation processes. The first two, the Franco-German reconciliation and the emergence of West Germany's autocritical *Vergangenheitsbewältigung*, had born fruit and considered successful by observers. These two processes were intertwined, as the changing rearticulation of German identity at home facilitated German political investment in reconciliation with its largest neighbour.[87] On the other hand, in the 1990s, the newly reunified German Federal Republic was undergoing a process of integration of the former German Democratic Republic into West German democratic structure. A substantial part of this process consisted in the purging of East German structures and confronting the immediate legacies of the SED dictatorship under the same vocabulary of 'dealing with the past'.[88] However, just as the new German state demonstrated extreme political will to confront the past as quickly as possible, later assessment of the integration

---

[85] David, 'The Emergence of the "Dealing with the Past" Agenda', p. 9.

[86] One example of German 'reconciliation' that has often been used as proof of German memory as a process of reconciliation is the Franco-German reconciliation as a mechanism of post-war transitional reconciliation. See Ackermann, Alice, 'Reconciliation as a Peace-Building Process in Post-War Europe'.

[87] See, for example, Rosoux, 'La réconciliation franco-allemande'.

[88] See, for example, Hammerstein, Mählert, Trappe and Wolfrum, 'Aufarbeitung der Diktatur – Diktat der Aufarbeitung?' and Suckut and Weber, *Stasi-Akten zwischen Politik und Zeitgeschichte*.

process of the East referred to it as a 'colonisation' by the West and a 'missed opportunity' due to Western triumphalism and exclusion of East German voices from the new reconstruction.[89] Consequently, as actors spoke of 'German successes' in international discussions over transitional justice, it became unclear which 'successes' they were drawing on. The high involvement of GDR dissidents like Joachim Gauck in transitional justice meetings highlighted a process occurring both in Germany and in international organisations: as policymakers were confronted with numerous global challenges of transition and democratisation, they sought to create quick blueprints for action that could be imposed from the top-down. In Germany, the desire to quickly implement a memory transformation of the East resulted in a popular backlash of the emergence of a narrative of nostalgia to East Germany as resistance to West German control of the new state.[90] Most notably, Western imposition of memorial structures that aimed at delegitimising the oppressive structures of the GDR did not allow space or time for the emergence of autocritical East German memory based on a narrative of introspection.

In the same vein, as international organisations sought to create a blueprint for 'best practice' to transform national narratives, they overlooked the main 'inconvenience' of the gestation and establishment of Germany's culture of autocritical memory: the rationale for 'remembering' the past had taken a long time to emerge through internal, national conversations. It was first articulated by intellectuals, and only later adopted by political actors in a way that was neither linear nor easily reproduced. Moreover, German memory's relation to international pressure was contradictory at best. On the one hand, (West) German intellectuals confronted the issue of 'dealing with the past' as an injunction to reintegrate a new Germany in a new international order and addressed how the eyes of the world were set on Germany. They predicated the relationship with the exterior world, however, on the acceptance of Germany's complete defeat in the Second World War, making it impossible for the new polity to make intellectual demands of the victors. On the other hand, conversations about the necessity to reinvent German democracy were internal in nature and did not involve international actors, but rather intellectual conversations about German democratisation and reinvention. The desire of international actors to 'streamline' the lengthy and non-linear internal processes into a set of actions that could be imposed from the top – and the outside – ignored the process of autocritical memory articulation for the goal of a desired outcome. Lea David has defined this type of outcome as 'moral remembrance', which prescribed focus on victims' narratives for the sake of social reconciliation

---

[89] Heitzer, Jander, Poutrus and Kahane, *Nach Auschwitz*.   [90] Bach, *What Remains*.

and an evolving discourse of human rights, which underpinned transition and democratisation.[91]

In David's definition of 'moral remembrance', she has critiqued the focus on victims in the search for justice. The first question transitional justice professionals were confronted with was how to define 'victims'. While the UN General Assembly's definition of a victim from 1985 opted for an inclusive category of persons who 'individually or collectively, have suffered harm [...] through acts or omissions that are in violation of criminal law',[92] memorialisation mechanisms created hierarchies of victims. Even as victims had different stories – and different ways of dealing with suffering, whether through choice to address suffering or desire to remain silent to not relive painful memories – the creation of a formulaic narrative of remembrance relied on 'representative' stories. While crimes could be generalised into a story of general responsibilities, creating a 'representative victim' inevitably flattened the experiences of victims. This created a competition between victims to claim the moral authority to speak as a 'pure victim'.[93] The moral imperative of victim-centred memorialisation thus created incentives for victims to engage in ongoing competition for official recognition. This contradicted the principle of memory as a healing mechanism in post-conflict societies. Moreover, while the focus on victims emerged from a moral desire for justice and reparation, it left less space to engage with the meaning of crimes for descendants of perpetrators.

The victim-focus therefore transformed the nuts and bolts of memory. Commemoration – and debates about history – turned to focus on the moral uprightness of victims rather than the perpetrators' crimes. Victims competed to show they were morally 'deserving' of a place in commemorative discourses. But in this process debates on memory lost sight of the fact that victims were commemorated not because of their specific moral goodness but because of crimes done to them by others. Moreover, the mixed borrowing from different 'models' into the transitional justice rationale only accentuated the contradictions of victim-focused commemorations in international settings. Transitional justice borrowed the moral argument for renewal from the German case, but the victim-focused public interaction from the Argentinian and South African cases. However, while confrontations between victims and perpetrators in Argentina and South Africa had been a national affair, in the case of German atrocities, victims and perpetrators (and their descendants) lived in separate

---

[91] See David, *The Past Can't Heal Us* and David, 'The Emergence of the "Dealing with the Past" Agenda'.

[92] UN General Assembly, *Declaration of Basic Principles of Justice for Victims of Crime and Abuse of Power*, Resolution 40/34, 29 November 1985.

[93] David, *The Past Can't Heal Us*, pp. 62–64.

states, where international mechanisms would have been more relevant for dialogue and reconciliation. In this one case, however, international coercion had been as good as absent. These contradictions fed into the articulation of the necessity to adopt ad-hoc mechanisms for international dialogue, which ignored the autocritical factor that had underlined the lengthy creation of German 'memory culture'. This lack of attention to autocritical memory became visible in the first European test case of transitional justice, as international organisations sought to implement the principles of transitional justice for the sake of peace and reconciliation in the Balkans after the Yugoslav Wars of the 1990s.

The next section explores the failure of transitional justice in Serbia as one of the 'test cases' of the new desire to create an actionable and global 'memory model'. The rise of memory as a concept that was detached from the historical specificities and material condition of its success and rearticulated into an abstract model of moral righteousness could not be introduced into any other national context. In Serbia as elsewhere, material conditions and historical specificities made it impossible to introduce a top-down model of memory that had neither the time to develop nor the anchoring in cultural and political elites to survive. The focus on abstract and victim-centred models also shifted the focus away from the original autocritical rationale.

2.2 The Case of Serbia: The Failure of the Memory Model

In the midst of much of the 'end of history' triumphalism of the 1990s, the Yugoslav Wars represented a challenge for international structures in bringing peace after the return of genocidal violence to the heart of Europe. From the breakaway of Slovenia, Macedonia (now North Macedonia) and Croatia from Yugoslavia in 1991 until NATO's intervention in 1995, the war ravaged the territories of the multi-ethnic south-eastern European state. It ended by an international agreement that ensured the emergence of new states defined by ethno-national definitions, most notably Croatia, Bosnia and Herzegovina (that the Dayton Agreement divided into the Bosniak-Croat Federation of Bosnia and Herzegovina [BiH] and the Serb Republika Srpska [RS]) and the state of Serbia and Montenegro, which would later see the breakaway of Montenegro.[94] The cessation of hostilities did not mean a return to peace and stability, however, as the new polities had been marked by the brutalisation of the war, and in the case of Bosnia a division into two antagonising entities. While all sides participated in the war, the war's violence did not affect all warring sides equally. Most of the fighting took place in Bosnia and parts of Croatia and involved numerous war crimes and acts of ethnic cleansing, the most staggering of which were the

---

[94] For a general history of the Yugoslav Wars, see Baker, *The Yugoslav Wars of the 1990s*.

systemic killings and rape of Bosniak Muslims by Bosnian Serb and Serbian troops. Serbian war crimes in Bosnia included the siege of Sarajevo and the use of camps, some for the internment and rape of Bosnian women. The most well-known crime was the massacre of over 8,000 Bosniak men and boys in Srebrenica in 1995, which the International Court in the Hague characterised as an act of genocide in 2004 and again in 2007.[95] The new toolkit of international justice became key in the management of the new polities and their democratisation. International actors sought to include memory mechanisms into politics of dialogue and reconciliation between the newly created states and recently separated ethnic groups.

The issue of 'memory', however, was just one component in the new system of transitional justice that was foreseen through some of the mechanisms of the Dayton Agreement, and which sought to engineer peaceful democratisation. International organisations sought to support democratic state building through a mix of incentives. These included peacebuilding programmes on the ground, sticks in the forms of pressures to comply with international demands of upholding democratic standards and a commitment to a process of 'Europeanisation' with possible EU membership as the ultimate carrot. As the notion of 'justice for victims' was so heavily intertwined with the objective of 'moving on', generously funded NGOs on the ground engaged in programmes of dialogue and reconciliation, while the newly founded International Criminal Tribunal for Yugoslavia (ICTY) was meant to deliver justice to the victims by putting war criminals on trial.[96]

These programmes attempted to quickly create the infrastructure for reconciliation through transitional justice's focus on 'best practice'. Simultaneously, however, they neglected the intellectual processes of narrative creation that underpinned the very meaning of memory. As former Yugoslavia separated into different states, each ethno-national community developed its own narrative of the war – and indeed of its relationship to pre-war Yugoslavia – to legitimise the new nationalist state structures.[97] Out of these new states, the case of Serbia was most relevant for the intersection between autocritical memory and the new mechanisms of transitional justice. Not only was Serbia (or the State of Serbia of Montenegro) the main belligerent state that sought to hold Yugoslavia together and carried the responsibility for the gravest war crimes during the

---

[95] On the Srebrenica genocide, see Cushman and Mestrovic, *This Time We Knew*, on the Hague rulings, see Subotić, *Hijacked Justice*, pp. 137–39.

[96] On the ongoing relationship between Serbia and the ICTY, see Peskin, *International Justice in Rwanda and the Balkans*, chs. 2–3.

[97] See David, *The Past Can't Heal Us*, pp. 103–107, but also Jović, *Rat i mit* and Prošić-Dvornic, 'Serbia: The Inside Story', pp. 317–38.

Yugoslav Wars (if by no means all crimes), these crimes were committed in the name of 'Greater Serbia'.[98] Creating narratives and structures of Serbian statehood thus required dealing with the role of Serbian perpetrators, and in so doing also with notions of 'responsibility' and 'accountability' on a greater scale. Here, and to a much greater degree than was the case in Germany, debates about Serbia's role in the war intersected with international pressures. The construction of a post-war Serbian identity became entangled with ideas of 'compliance' and 'resistance' to outside pressure.

While international actors' desire to support democratisation in the Balkans and in Serbia was attached to the recent formulation of transitional justice principles that translated into top-down mechanisms, the energy for articulation of 'responsibility' required internal social and intellectual autocritical engagement. In the 1990s, as the country remained under the full control of its wartime leader Slobodan Milošević, Serbian society did not experience a moment of full rupture from former governments like in Germany or Argentina. Similarly, it did not experience the growth of home-grown structures that needed to legitimise radical transitions. Skirting around this contradiction, the main issue that became a marker of all new states' compliance with top-down international measures of justice thus quickly became governments' readiness to cooperate with the ICTY. International aid and support followed Serbian willingness to deliver war criminals to justice in the Hague. Under Milošević, cooperation between Serbian authorities and the ICTY was scarce to non-existent. Only after his ousting in 2000, which opened the door for the promise of rewards from the US and EU, did subsequent Serbian governments begin a process of engagement with the ICTY's demands.[99] For the process of engagement with the past – or with Serbian identity for that matter – Milošević's ousting did not entail a process of transformation of the country's ruling elite and structures, and did not usher an elite desire to legitimate a new Serbian and Montenegrin state in opposition to the crimes of the former. Instead, the political transition was framed as a bare necessity to comply with international pressures. This foresaw a dynamic of cat and mouse between international organisations and Serbian governments.

As Subotić points out, international organisations did not have a consistent policy towards Serbia other than expecting war criminals to be sent to the Hague, while Serbian governments tried to stall as much as possible in

---

[98] Crowe, *War Crimes, Genocide and Justice*, pp. 342–45 and Radović, 'Yugoslav Wars and Some of Their Social Consequences', pp. 25–68.

[99] Peskin, *International Justice in Rwanda and the Balkans*, pp. 29–60.

delivering war criminals to the ICTY.[100] In dealing with international actors, Serbian governments' willingness to comply depended on the carrot and stick available to them. In the catastrophic financial state Serbia found itself after the Milošević years, the main carrots on offer were the release of well-needed financial aid or the possibility of accession to the EU or the Council of Europe. Despite any expectations that Serbian governments would embrace transition – and the jurisdiction of the international court – as a way to demarcate a clear rupture with the Milošević era, this did not occur. Patchy Serbian compliance reflected a desire to only go after Serbian war criminals when there was no other choice available.

One example for the relationship between international coercion, Serbian half-measures and the presumed goal of Serbian introspection was the ongoing back-and-forth on the arrest and extradition of the Bosnian Serb wartime leader Radovan Karadžić, who had become one of Europe's best-known fugitives from justice for charges of genocide, crimes against humanity and war crimes against the non-Serb population of Bosnia and Herzegovina. Consecutive Serbian governments continuously claimed they had no information of his whereabouts and used various stalling tactics – including the delivery of less prominent war criminals – to try and appease international demands to deliver Karadžić as proof of facing the country's own crimes. It was only in 2008, with a change of Serbian government and increased international pressures, that Karadžić, by then reincarnated as a spiritual healer in a suburb of Belgrade after thirteen years in hiding, was captured on a Belgrade commuter bus and extradited to the Hague. The government's explanation for finally arresting Karadžić, however, did not address any of the rationales of autocritical memory. Instead of an opportunity to incite a debate about the meaning of war crimes for Serbian identity in the present, the government addressed the arrest as, in the words of Serbia's defence minister, 'a step towards European integration', or compliance with 'foreign' western demands.[101]

Simultaneously, for the internal Serbian debate, extraditions of war criminals had become a main political fault line. Here again, debates about cooperation with the ICTY did not reflect a social engagement with responsibility to Serbian crimes, but rather a desire to protect the Serbian nation from external threats. Any expectation that new governments would just enthusiastically embrace autocritical 'facing the past' without any heavy social contestation was naïve and did not square with any previous experiences, particularly as discussions of war crimes affected the immediate experiences of the war generation, rather than

---

[100] Subotić, *Hijacked Justice*, pp. 42–45 and Peskin, *International Justice in Rwanda and the Balkans*, pp. 61–92.

[101] Quoted in Subotić, *Hijacked Justice*, p. 2.

the German or French examples of a second generation that confronted their parents' record. Moreover, the Serbian political elite remained roughly the same as in the Milošević years. Serbian political decision makers did not face transition as an opportunity – and a need – to delegitimate the previous regime to establish clear distinction and articulate new political identities, unlike the West German or Argentinian examples. The issue of extraditions quickly became a marker of political identities and fights in Serbia, as conservative actors like President Vojislav Koštunica (president 2000–3, prime minister 2004–7) articulated a narrative of defending Serbian 'heroes' against international demands of the Hague. For a while, the reformist Prime Minister Zoran Đinđić (prime minister 2000–3) represented a Serbian 'Europeanised' identity through his extradition of Milošević to 'increase Serbia's international prestige'.[102] This focus on international compliance was instrumental at best and did not reflect a desire to engage with Serbian responsibility. And yet, even Đinđić's openness to practical cooperation with the Hague, and the potential for more enthusiastic cooperation that could have further emerged, was quickly nipped in the bud. His assassination in 2003 by the group Red Berets in an operation called 'Stop the Hague', paved the way for the establishment of nationalist politicians in Serbia's political elite.

For Serbian society therefore, the continuous handwringing over trials in the Hague made it impossible for trials to become what transitional justice actors intended them to be: markers of consensus over a specific responsibility of the Serbian leadership for the crimes of the Yugoslav wars. Instead, the constant conflict paved the way for the strengthening of a narrative of Serbian victimhood facing international pressures. While it was comparable to the 'poor Germany' narrative that transpired much of the public conversation in West Germany of the 1950s, the Serbian elite's active resistance to international pressures contributed to the creation of an additional layer of this narrative, as nationalist actors mobilised an image of Serbian 'heroes of the nation' against international targeting of Serbia. Serbian governments did not avoid dealing with the past like postwar governments in Germany, but mobilised the conflict with international institutions to create of a narrative of victimisation. Furthermore, many Serbian intellectuals, like the international award-winning film-maker Emir Kosturica or the novelist Momo Kapor, began articulating nationalist narratives about Serbian heroism facing international oppression.[103] The alignment of prominent intellectuals with the Serbian state reflected another narrative of national cohesion against international actors, which weakened further actors in Serbia who called for facing Serbian responsibility.[104]

---

[102] *Nedeljni telegraf*, 9 May 2001.

[103] See, for example, an interview with Kosturica on RTV, 17 April 2007.

[104] See Subotić, *Hijacked Justice*, pp. 66–69 on the failures on domestic power from below.

Beyond handwringing about trials, the government's control of much of the Serbian narrative became evident, however, in debates about the genocide in Srebrenica and particularly in the Serbian tape affair. In 2005, the prosecution in Slobodan Milošević's case uncovered a video tape that showed Serbian sparatroopers from Serbia proper torturing and executing six young Bosniak men, while a Serbian Orthodox priest was giving his blessing to the paramilitaries. The shock value of the video evidence elicited emotional condemnations in the media and the police arrested the perpetrators identified on the tape. The emotional outrage lasted only a few days, however, as government officials were quick to provide counter-narratives to prevent any national reckoning with Srebrenica as a specifically Serbian crime. These included a focus on the individual perpetrators as deranged, or in the words of the Serbian minister of the interior Dragan Jočić 'infantile',[105] dismissals of Serbia's responsibility for events in Bosnia (despite the tape's portrayal of Serbians rather than Bosnian Serbs), calls to place Srebrenica in a context in which all sides had committed war crimes and lastly, claiming that the focus on Srebrenica was exaggerated and only reflected an international hatred of Serbia. The state of the public debate showed that popular sentiment in Serbia was not ready to, in the words of Nenad Dimitrijević, 'publicly acknowledge facts that were privately known'.[106] Debating the past in Serbia did not initiate popular reckoning with Serbian responsibility, but ended in political affirmation of Serbian victimisation against belligerent international institutions. Unlike the cases of West Germany and France, where the decades after the Second World War were characterised by silence, failed international attempts to hold Serbia responsible did not foster an autocritical culture that gained popular support to challenge elite nationalist discourse. The conflict between international pressure and national resistance did not diminish over time.[107]

The Serbian case demonstrates the limits of the political processes that leverage international pressure to shape processes of reckoning on a national level. The prescriptive policies of international courts and memory activists who wished to implement 'tried and tested' ways to incite public debates failed to engage Serbian elites and the society at large. While policies offered institutional backing, these did not offer alternatives for a reinvention of Serbian identity. Despite the best wishes to engage Serbia in international 'dialogue',

---

[105] Ćurgus Kazimir, 'Jevreji, trgovke belim robljem i škorpioni'.

[106] Dimitrijević, 'Serbia after the Criminal Past', pp. 5–22 (p. 5). See also Obradović-Wochnik, 'The "Silent Dilemma" of Transitional Justice', pp. 328–47.

[107] See here for example the incident in 2015, as the Serbian nationalist President Aleksandar Vučić was pelted with stones by angry Bosnian demonstrators at the official commemoration in Srebrenica and capitalised on the incident at home to show Serbian victimhood. See, for example, David, *The Past Can't Heal Us*, p. 114.

debates about the meaning of the war were framed by national questions. Lea David thus points out that while the many NGOs that emerged through generous international backing for the sake of creating encounters and micro-solidarity programmes engaged in numerous exchanges between Bosniaks, Croats and Serbs of all ages, these made a very small dent in national discourse and were 'hijacked by the state'.[108]

The Serbian case marks a failure to establish dominant autocritical narratives in the aftermath of conflict. On the one hand, this is not surprising, as autocritical memory was not a 'natural' model. The Serbian difficulties of prioritising narratives of 'responsibility' or 'coming to terms with the past' so shortly after the end of the Yugoslav Wars were not entirely specific for Serbia, as even West Germany of the 1950s did not yet offer fertile grounds for engagement with autocriticism. On the other hand, however, the Serbian case is important as one of the first post-conflict cases of international pressures on states to democratise through mechanisms of transitional justice, including focus on memory.

The Serbian case shows that even as international actors began believing in the universality of values like 'coming to terms with the past', these did not automatically translate into national contexts through the toolkit of transitional justice. To some extent, this was the result of the inability to translate a supposedly universalist model into a regional context with its own specificities. In this case, nationalist groups remained dominant in the new Serbian state and were not interested in legitimising a new democratic state through the discrediting of the Milošević regime.

Moreover, inconsistent and unfocused international pressures became a hindrance to the creation of autocritical memory narratives they sought to support. Firstly, the focus on trials as the main, if not only, component of 'dealing with the past' neglected the importance of internal intellectual engagement with the meaning of responsibility for Serbia. The lack of state and high-ranking intellectual desire to promote democratisation through responsibility could not be compensated by small-scale grassroots attempts to foster empathy with victims. International hopes for change through grassroots 'encounters' did not establish any counter-narrative either, as participants who connected to one another on an individual level returned to the safety of their homes and had no alternative autocritical discourse that allowed them to rearticulate their political identities. Secondly, and just as importantly, international pressures engendered resistance of national elites – both political and intellectual – who doubled down on a narrative of national victimisation, which they promoted through the power of the state and media. With a lack of focus on any reason to

---

[108] David, *The Past Can't Heal Us*, pp. 166–71.

accept responsibility as perpetrators, Serbian intellectuals and decision makers turned to narratives of victimisation to articulate nationalist Serbian identities following the breakup of Yugoslavia. Ultimately, the Serbian case demonstrates David's, Gensburger's and Lefranc's arguments that the focus on the suffering of victims does not in itself support the creation of a moral or empathic memory.[109] Neglecting the focus on the transformation of perpetrators made it even more difficult to create any autocritical memory as a base of new democratic renewal.

2.3 The Jedwabne Debate: Transitioning into Europe?

While commentators have characterised Serbia's transition into democracy as problematic at best, observers by the end of the first decade of the 2000s celebrated Poland as a democratic success story in Eastern-Central Europe.[110] These observations held at least until the return of the far-right populist party Prawo i Sprawiedliwość (Law and Justice, PiS) to power in 2015, as new governments harnessed the power of the state to undermine liberal-democratic institutions and norms.[111] The Jedwabne debate that raged in Poland in the early 2000s reflected the role of autocritical memory in the articulation of Polish identities as a European liberal-democratic polity.

In 2000, the Polish American (and Jewish) author Jan Tomasz Gross published a short book called *Neighbours*. The book described the massacre of the quasi entirety of the Jewish population of one small town in the east of Poland, Jedwabne, by their Polish neighbours in 1941.[112] Just over a decade after the fall of communism, the publication of the book triggered the biggest public debate to date in democratic Poland that tied 'facing the past' with the articulation of new cosmopolitan Polish identities in a transition into democracy. The debate involved numerous actors and contrasted two different kinds of memory: a victimised Polish national memory with an autocritical narrative. The clash between nationalist narratives of Polish victimhood and an autocritical narrative of 'moving on' reflected two sides in Poland's transition into a democracy in the heart of the European Union (EU). Contestations of memory narratives about the role of Poles during the Second World War became entangled with reinvention and rearticulation of Polish identities in Europe.

---

[109] Gensburger and Lefranc, *A quoi servent les politiques de mémoire?* and David, *The Past Can't Heal Us*.

[110] See, for example, Piatkowski, *Poland's New Golden Age*.

[111] See, for example, Bernhard, 'Democratic Backsliding in Poland and Hungary', and Holesch and Kyriazi, 'Democratic Backsliding in the European Union', pp. 1–20.

[112] Gross, *Sąsiedzi*.

The main theme that *Neighbours* raised was that of Polish crimes against Jews during the Holocaust, and thus Polish responsibility. It was not the first time that Polish intellectuals addressed the issue of Polish animosity to Jews and complicity in the Nazi genocide, or in the words of Jan Błoński, 'insufficient concern' for the fate of their Jewish neighbours.[113] Gross' book, however, described a case that entirely challenged national narratives about Polish righteous suffering in the Second World War. Using testimonies of one of the only survivors from Jedwabne together with further archival material, Gross revealed how the Polish inhabitants of an ordinary town massacred the near totality of their Jewish neighbours. More shockingly to readers, they did so without any orders or even persuasion from German occupiers in what was a series of such massacres in eastern Polish towns.

The publication of *Neighbours* triggered a relentless two-year long debate on the pages of all Polish media outlets that involved the entirety of the country's political, intellectual and religious elite as well as an incessant outpour of letters from 'ordinary' Poles who commented Jedwabne and the ongoing debate.[114] While none could dismiss the fact that Poles had murdered their Jewish neighbours, the debate quickly formed two camps, a nationalist 'defensive' camp that rejected any generalisation of guilt beyond individual 'criminals', and another calling for national reckoning with the meaning of Jedwabne for contemporary Polish society.[115]

In both cases, the questions of 'Polish guilt' and the view of the Polish nation was central to arguments about remembering Jedwabne in the present. Conservative actors aimed to relativise the meaning of the killings through claims of either German involvement or the claims that Jews were no 'pure victims', as their supposed collaboration with Soviet forces that had occupied Jedwabne between 1939 and 1941 had made Polish retaliation 'understandable'. Conservative historians like Bogdan Musiał and Tomasz Strzembosz thus found flaws with Gross' methodology, argued that his claim of 1,600 Jewish victims was inflated and thus a sign of botched research (which led to a mass exhumation of bodies in Jedwabne), and sought proof of German involvement in the killings.[116] But the main argument of conservative intellectuals, journalists, clergymen and letters to newspapers was that it was impossible for the 'glorious' Polish nation, that had been forged through suffering, to contemplate collective guilt. In so doing, arguments against guilt repeated a narrative of double Polish victimisation and occupation by Nazi Germany and the Soviet

---

[113] Błoński, 'Biedni Polacy patrzą na getto'.

[114] Törnquist-Plewa, 'The Jewdwabne Killings', pp. 141–74.

[115] Michlic, *Coming to Terms with the 'Dark Past'*.

[116] See, for example, Strzembosz, 'Z jednej okupacji pod drugą', and Musiał, 'Nie wolno się bać'.

Union, joined by international victimisation through portrayal of Poland as inherently antisemitic.[117] In so doing, many commentators reproduced an anti-semitic narrative of Jewish world domination, as they condemned a supposed international pressure on Poland to apologise as an international Jewish con-spiracy and 'Holocaust business' that allows Jews to claim victimisation over Poles, thus continuing a supposed Jewish support of Soviet crimes against Poles.

For Polish liberals writing on the pages of newspapers like *Gazeta Wyborcza*, *Rzeczpospolita* and *Więź*, the self-image of Poles as eternal victims was a hindrance to reckoning with the long legacy of Polish antisemitism and the improvement of Polish–Jewish relations. Indeed, Gross' call on Polish society to finally properly 'mourn its Jewish victims' addressed the debate as a moral issue that would lead to possible reconciliation.[118] The power of the Jedwabne debate for Polish liberal journalists and intellectuals like Joanna Tokarska-Bakir or Adam Michnik, however, also emerged from the idea of using autocritical memory as a tool for transition into a mature, non-nationalist European democ-racy, as one editorial entitled 'Standing on the Side of Truth' in the influential left-leaning newspaper Gazeta Wyborcza claimed:

> Poland is today the only post-Communist country which has dared such a confrontation with its history and its shame [...] All this shows that Polish democracy is on the road of truth and that truth serves democracy. We deserve a place in the community of free nations. There are reasons for other nations to view Poland with respect.[119]

Interpreting the ability to 'deal with the past' as a sign of pride in a new Polish identity reflected the role of the Jedwabne debate in Polish internal debates about transition and delegitimisation of the Communist past as a period with no 'mature' and free public sphere. Linking Jedwabne with debates about the shape of Poland new democracy served to explain some of the force and acrimony of public engagement with this issue in this exact period. In a period of stabilisa-tion after the economic hardship of the 1990s, a greater number of actors became concerned with a Europeanisation of Polish society, access to the EU and the reshaping of Polish identities. For liberals in Poland, then, autocritical memory became a sign of fighting against an 'old' spectre of Polish nationalism for the sake of creating pride in an 'open', European identity. The then liberal Polish government mobilised the image of autocritical Poles in international settings, like the speech the Polish Foreign Minister Władysław Bartoszewski held in front of the World Jewish Congress in the US in 2001, where he

---

[117] See, for example, Macierewicz, 'Rewolucja nihilizmu'.
[118] Gross, 'Zrozumiałe morderstwo?'.   [119] *Gazeta Wyborcza*, 10 July 2001.

described the Jedwabne debate as an opportunity for the Polish state to face its own past for the sake of future reconciliation.[120]

As the then president Aleksander Kwaśniewski went to apologise in a highly mediatised ceremony in Jedwabne in July 2001, it seemed that autocritical memory had become a new Polish state principle. In the following years, however, new governments and debates showed that the Jedwabne debate had not ended with an autocritical consensus. New conservative and far-right actors in Poland, amongst which were the recurrently ruling party Law and Justice (PiS) or the far-right League of Polish Families with its conservative Catholic radio station Radio Maryja, mobilised the narrative of Polish victimisation and resistance to supposed international pressure to adopt a Western European identity that included reckoning with Polish crimes. Particularly after the reelection of PiS in 2015, Polish memorial politics became even more belligerent, focusing on Polish resistance to the double occupation by Nazi Germany and the Soviet Union. The Polish state controlled public media and right-wing tabloids repeatedly accused German actors – and particularly those seen as liberal like the conservative Chancellor Angela Merkel or the EU politician Ursula von der Leyen – as revictimising Poland, as they portrayed European criticism of the Polish government's attacks on the rule of law and separation of powers as a culture war between left-wing Europe and the Polish nation.[121] PiS governments thus repeatedly accused international actors for wanting to 'falsify' history through expectations Poland reckoned with its past. In so doing, right-wing political elites mobilised memory politics again, as they claimed international actors were using the term 'Polish concentration camps' not as a geographical description of camps that had been built by the Nazis in Poland, but as means to attack Polish reputation and accuse Poles of responsibility for the Holocaust. In 2018, the Polish government mobilised the debate on Polish concentration camps to criminalise any public statements ascribing the Polish nation collective responsibility for Holocaust related crimes.[122]

Between the Jedwabne debate and the 2018 law that outlawed critical reflection about Polish responsibility for crimes in the Holocaust, Polish society continuously engaged with autocritical memory as a component in the construction of Polish democracy. While the Jedwabne debate was an internal Polish debate that confronted various actors in Poland with Polish responsibility for crimes against Polish Jews, both the debate and its aftermath reflected an understanding of autocritical memory as an international expectation, and

---

[120] Törnquist-Plewa, 'The Jewdwabne Killings', p. 164.

[121] See, for example, *Wprost*, 10 January 2016.

[122] See Soroka and Krawatzek, 'Nationalism, Democracy, and Memory Laws', pp. 157–71 and Hackmann, 'Defending the "Good Name" of the Polish Nation', pp. 587–606.

thus became a bone of contention in imagining Poland's position in the world. Just like in Serbia, right-wing actors portrayed resistance to auto criticism as resistance to international imposition, even though no international mechanisms pressurised Polish governments to come to terms with its past. For liberal actors, autocritical memory reflected compliance with international norms of 'proper' remembrance and a way to forge a European identity through transition. As these two world views got increasingly entrenched, the recurrent and acrimonious debates about reckoning with Poland's dark past reflected both the power of international expectations to 'remember' the past and their potential to ignite nationalist backlash.

2.4 Conclusion: Memory, Justice and Democratisation

In the 1990s, following the third wave of democratisation and with the transition of Eastern European states into democracy, both international and national actors sought mechanisms to manage polities' transitions. In a globalised environment shaped by the atrocities of the twentieth century, democracy became increasingly viewed as a solution to hinder the repetition of these crimes. Based on the success of post-war German democracy amongst others, international actors viewed 'dealing with the past' as a formula that would foster democratic values through 'proper' remembrance of the past. Yet, while trying to create universal models based on the logic of crimes against humanity, international actors were confronted with the contradictions between universal abstract rejection of atrocities and the historical specificities of their gestation. In so doing, they formulated 'best practice' mechanisms that were based on ahistorical understanding of 'success stories' that sought to bring justice through healing and reconciliation. For the long-term functioning of justice, justice and truth telling mechanisms sought the creation of the 'proper' kind of memory, which would confront the societies of perpetrators with crimes committed in their name and lead to autocritical reflections. Even more importantly, through recognition of the long-standing collective 'wounds' and trauma that remained in victim societies, these mechanisms sought to elevate the voices of victims to confront perpetrators' societies through demands for understanding and empathy.

While each and every one of these principles is laudable in and of itself, transitional justice mechanisms and the many incentives to prioritise 'proper' remembrance have not delivered the results memory actors of the 1990s hoped for. These models' focus on the universality of moral demands – often based on the elevation of victims and their voices – clashed with regional and national specificities, where different actors mobilised memory for their own objectives.

The cases of Serbia and Poland demonstrate how actors in both countries were aware of memory's ascendancy on the international stage, as Serbian actors reacted to actual international pressures, or as Polish liberals referred to Europeans' eyes set on the Jedwabne debate.

In both cases, however, awareness to the world did not necessarily translate to embracing either David's 'moral remembrance' or clear autocritical narratives. In both cases, memory debates became tools in internal struggles to define national narratives in moments of transition. As autocritical narratives required acknowledging and discrediting national complicity with previous crimes, they served actors whose intent was to legitimise new identities rather than continuities. In this vein, Serbian state structures hijacked memorial debates about crimes of the war and replaced them with national narratives about Serbian victimisation. In Poland, conservative actors mobilised narratives of national victimisation to portray a continuity with an 'eternal Poland', while liberal actors harnessed the promise of autocritical memory to paint a picture of a European Poland that reinvented for the sake of 'moving on'. In both cases, autocritical memory's failure to create a consensus reflected the lack of consensus about what 'moving on' meant and what kind of future actors promised their constituencies.

3 Autocritical Memory and the Crimes of Empire: Can Memory Achieve Racial Justice?

In June 2020, just as the first wave of Covid-19 lockdowns were easing in Europe, crowds of protesters poured into streets of different European cities. They were prompted by of the murder of George Floyd by police officers in the US and the ensuing protests under the banner of Black Lives Matter (BLM). While Western European protesters mobilised against analogous concerns to their North American ones – including police violence, racial profiling and other forms of systemic racism – some demonstrations became notable for targeting local visible traces of colonial domination. These included the toppling of the statue of philanthropist and slave trader Edward Colston in Bristol in the UK,[123] the targeting of monuments to King Leopold II in Belgian cities[124] or Portuguese associations of Afro-descendants calling to face the country's legacy of empire and racism.[125] Demonstrators all over different ex-colonising European countries engaged in a simultaneous 'BLM moment', in which reactions to racism in the US ignited debates about Europe's colonial past and

---

[123] *The Guardian*, 07 June 2020.

[124] Goddereis, 'Black Lives Matter in Belgium (June 2020)', www.rosalux.eu/en/article/1796 .black-lives-matter-in-belgium-june-july-2020.html (last accessed on 23 February 2023).

[125] *Publico*, 6 June 2020.

connected memory politics with fighting racism. Nonetheless, engagement with the memory of empire began far earlier than 2020, and it happened unevenly in different European contexts, depending on national and international circulations of ideas about memory and available models of memory politics.

This section examines the emergence of memory debates about empire in France and Germany and their relation to race and existing autocritical models. The wave of simultaneous contestation of empire reflected a new embrace of memory politics by antiracist activists and intellectuals. Many of these actors did not admit they were addressing 'memory' as such, but claimed to be harnessing history to explain the salience of racism in contemporary societies. This section demonstrates how the availability of 'memory vocabulary' through intellectual and political engagement with memory – and not least autocritical memory – reached activists at a moment of economic and social crisis, as they needed new strategies to fight racism. Simultaneously, however, the new primacy of memory politics, which had emerged from the so-called success of autocritical memory in France and Germany, did not reflect the desire to replicate that model, but critique it.

3.1 From a Duty to Remember to Memory Wars in France

3.1.1 The Road to 2005: Harnessing the Duty to Remember to Address Colonial History

France was the first European country to experience a sustained public and political debate about the memory of empire that has raged on several fronts since the 1990s. By the 2010s it had become so ubiquitous that even the Ministry of Education added the 'Memory of the Algerian War' (rather than just its history) to the list of obligatory themes for the baccalaureate exam – or high school leaving certificate – in history.[126] This was the result of a process of political mobilisation of the memory of colonialism by different actors, who appropriated the autocritical model of the 'Duty to remember'. While these 'memory actors'[127] – antiracist activists, intellectuals, historians and politicians – addressed different facets of empire, they always returned to the rationale of remembrance as a way of holding the state accountable for its 'duty' to its citizens. They used available memory vocabulary that called on the state to remember its own crimes to address their grievances in the present, most often

---

[126] Ministère de l'éducation nationale, *éduscol: ressources pour le lycée général et technologique*, Histoire Série S (2014) accessible online on: https://cache.media.eduscol.education.fr/file/lycee/12/3/01_RESS_LYC_HIST_TermS_th1_309123.pdf (last accessed on 23 February 2023).

[127] 'Memory actors' here will be a term for any public actors who participate in the creation of a memory narrative or a discourse.

to speak of the position of racialised communities in present-day postcolonial French society.

The 1990s saw the first contestations of colonial memory in France on two fronts: the memory of enslavement of Africans in the French colonies and the memory of the Algerian War of Independence. The first was the fruit of labour of Antillean activists in the French metropole, who sought to address the place of Caribbean French citizens in the republic. The French Antilles were France's oldest colonies, established in the sixteenth century in the phase of European expansion in the Americas and shaped by the enslavement of Africans. Unlike other colonies, however, they never gained independence but underwent a process of departmentalisation that affirmed their attachment to France.[128] By the 1990s, Caribbean activists in the Hexagon shifted from fighting for independence and began looking for new ways to make sense of their belonging to France, leading to a focus on the role of colonial slavery in forging Creole Caribbean communities and tying them to contemporary France. In this way, they turned to the newly minted memory vocabulary of 'Duty to remember' to raise awareness to the issue of enslavement.[129]

The accepted model of 'Duty to remember' was central to the very choice of Caribbean activists to define their activism through memory as much as it was for their political successes. The most notable early memory activists in France in the 1990s, the couple Serge and Viviane Romana, centred their activism on linking slavery to the development of Caribbean French identity through inspiration from and discussion with Jewish colleagues about trauma after the Holocaust.[130] The Romanas soon realised that they needed to address the link between slavery and the French citizenship of Caribbeans to make sense of present-day conditions. The French state's plan to commemorate the 150th anniversary of the abolition of slavery in 1998 gave them an opportunity to address the memory of enslavement in public through a large protest against the official commemoration's focus on an abolitionist narrative in a way that overshadowed French responsibility for the crimes of enslavement. This first large protest march became a symbolic cornerstone in the history of Caribbean mobilisation for the memory of slavery in France. It forced government actors to look for legal projects that would appease the Caribbean community through recognition of the French dimension of slavery. The government ended by tasking a young Socialist – and former independentist – MP from French

---

[128] For works on the French context of enslavement of Africans, see Cottias, La traite et les esclavages.

[129] See Chivallon, *L'esclavage, du souvenir à la mémoire*, on how Caribbean activists had previously used this vocabulary in the DOMs, but not in mainland France.

[130] Lotem, 'Between Resistance and the State', pp. 126–48 (128).

Guiana, Christiane Taubira (born 1952), with placating France's Caribbean communities. On 10 May 2001, Taubira succeeded in passing a law that became the cornerstone of what came to be called French 'memorial legislation' and was often seen as shaped on the example of the 1990 Gayssot Law that outlawed Holocaust denial. The 'Taubira Law' recognised the Atlantic slave trade as a crime against humanity, stipulated that it should receive the 'place it deserved' in school curricula and be institutionally commemorated with the help of a committee of experts.[131]

The 'Duty to remember' was a key to Taubira's successful campaign to appeal to the republic's 'soul' through President Chirac's autocritical precedent. Taubira not only received the unanimous support of the National Assembly on 10 May 2001. Three years later, a newly appointed committee chose 10 May, or the day of the unanimous passing of the Taubira Law, as a national Memorial Day for the slave trade, slavery and their abolitions.[132] Caribbean politicians achieved another memorial goal: integrating slavery in the national calendar, thus recognising the importance of admitting the responsibility of the French state for the slave trade. Caribbean activists thus harnessed the autocritical Duty to remember as a way of imposing a debate about the memory of enslavement. For them, remembering slavery was not necessarily always about the history of enslavement but their connection to contemporary France. Through their successful memory campaign they showed the way to other minorities whose voices were ignored by republican structures: autocritical memory was a tool that could be harnessed to frame other priorities.

Similarly, the Duty to remember gained ever greater salience through the activity of historians and activists who sought to focus the public debate in France on the importance of the Algerian War of Independence (1954–62), possibly the most violent war of European decolonisation, for French history and identity. The most notable of these actors was the historian Benjamin Stora, whose mission since the 1980s became to 'break the silence' on the Algerian War. In 1991, he published his influential book '*La gangrène et l'oubli*' and aired his documentary '*Les années algériennes*', both of which turned out to be defining moments in French debates about the memory of colonialism. For Stora, French society needed to face the wounds of Algeria to 'heal' as a nation. Stora borrowed heavily from the Vichy debate and was later quoted to having sought to produce the next 'Sorrow and the Pity', or a film that confronts ordinary French people with their colonial past in the same way as they had

---

[131] Lotem, 'Between Resistance and the State', pp. 126–48 (128).

[132] Lotem, 'Between Resistance and the State', p. 134, see also Lotem, *The Memory of Colonialism in Britain and France*, p. 129.

confronted the collaborationist past.[133] For Stora, the fact that there had been recurrent public debates about the Algerian War of Independence, particularly about the French military's extensive use of torture, did not amount to true 'remembering'. The historian claimed that true 'memory' required state acknowledgement of its own crimes – in the same way it had done for Vichy.[134]

Stora's argument on 'coming to terms' with the Algerian history was that the Algerian War of Independence was central to the French present, not only through the many traumas it had left with different groups, whether war veterans, Algerian immigrants, European settlers or Algerian auxiliary Muslims who had been forced out of Algeria after the war, but also through continuities with contemporary anti-Arab racism. While Stora's work was aimed at a left-wing audience that had already appropriated the Duty to remember through debates about Vichy, his argument was about the state. He claimed that public interest in the war, which was notable through the many films and books published about the war, meant very little without state acknowledgement. The fact that French governments had never acknowledged that the 'events' that had taken place in Algeria had been a war rather than a policing operation made the war 'nameless' (une guerre sans nom) and could thus not be properly 'remembered'.[135]

Stora's argument reflected a French specialty of privileging state mechanisms, which was also evident in the French autocritical model of Duty to remember. In 1999, however, as the French National Assembly acknowledged that the Algerian War of Independence had indeed been a war, the inclusion of the Algerian War into a French autocritical memory occurred through public debates that stirred public emotions. In particular, the trial of Maurice Papon in 1998 became a moment of public attention to the continuities between Vichy collaboration and colonial violence. Papon was put on trial for his role in the deportation of Jews during the Second World War, but the prosecution addressed his responsibility for the 17 October 1961 massacre of Algerian demonstrators in Paris as the Paris police prefect.[136] The trial embodied Stora's argument about the necessity to integrate the memory of Algerian violence into the French national narrative, if only for the sake of making sense of personal continuities between the two events. Only two years later, the violence of the war returned to the headlines, as the influential daily *Le Monde* published the account of an elderly Algerian woman, Louisette

---

[133] Branche, *La Guerre d'Algérie, une histoire apaisée?* p. 92.

[134] Stora, Benjamin, Les Années algériennes, TV Documentary. Ina/France2, 1991, and Stora, *La gangrène et l'oubli*.

[135] Stora, *La gangrène et l'oubli*, but see also Stora, *Le Transfert d'une mémoire*.

[136] On 17 October 1961 and its memory, see House and MacMaster, *Paris 1961*.

Ighilahriz, who had been tortured during the war, but was searching for the military doctor who had saved her life. The article confronted French society, that had grown accustomed to debates about torture, with a human story of an elderly Algerian woman, or a voice that had otherwise been absent from debates in France. It triggered an emotional public debate about torture in Algeria that stayed in the media for months.[137] The torture debate proved that the public in France cared about the Algerian War. As stories of veterans and other examples of torture came out into the open, it not only became impossible to deny the use of torture in Algeria but the debate also proved Stora's point that the war was important for French national consciousness. In a political discourse that had already been shaped by the importance of the Duty to remember, these debates showed how different actors were able to demand to include new stories in a memory discourse that defined national identity.[138]

3.1.2 Memory in France after 2005: From Memory Wars to Talking about Race

The moment that united the different strands of 'dealing with the past' into a general debate about the memory of colonialism in France was the year 2005, as different events coalesced into a snowball effect of public and political debates about France's colonial history. The main such event was the ongoing debate over the 23 February 2005 law. The law had emerged from *pied-noir* activists' lobbying, who had fashioned their goals on that of Jewish and Caribbean activists, and wanted a memorial law that recognised European settlers from North Africa as victims who should benefit from the republic's Duty to remember.[139] As the bill passed through preliminary debates in the National Assembly and the Senate, which were characterised by broad acceptance of its memorial idea (despite the absence of left-wing deputies in the initial hearing), the law emerged with an additional Article 4, which stipulated that school curricula focused on the 'positive role' of French overseas presence, or of French colonialism.[140] In passing a law that glorified French colonialism after a decade of debates about the need to discuss colonial crimes in France, the government not only proved Stora's thesis of French official 'forgetting' of colonial crimes but also demonstrated that the principle of Duty to remember

---

[137] Lotem, *The Memory of Colonialism in Britain and France*, pp. 77–80 and Cohen, 'The Sudden Memory of Torture', pp. 82–94.

[138] See also Lotem, 'The Road to 2005', pp. 324–39.

[139] Lotem, *The Memory of Colonialism in Britain and France*, pp. 160–67 and Eldridge, *From Empire to Exile*.

[140] Lotem, *The Memory of Colonialism in Britain and France*, pp. 160–67 and Liauzu and Mançeron (eds.), *La colonisation, la loi et l'histoire*.

was also open to be abused by different groups that sought recognition as victims. The ambiguous position of European settlers as both beneficiaries of French colonial policies and victims displaced by Algerian independence that facilitated *pied-noir* associations' appeal to the principle of *Devoir de mémoire*.

Nonetheless, growing protest against the law's Article 4, not least by Aimé Césaire, the previous anticolonial intellectual who had become a politician in Martinique, and the Algerian President Abdelaziz Bouteflika, forced the government to react. While Conservative UMP deputies refused to budge on the law, Socialist deputies demanded to rescind the law's Article 4.[141] The parliamentary debate on the law was set for November and took place just after the October riots in French cities. These were triggered by the electrocution of two young Maghrebi boys fleeing the police and thus became a symbol for the French 'malaise', or the effects of decades of neglect, segregation and systemic racism in the French suburbs. As a result, debates on the law linked the glorification of colonialism – and thus the theme of its remembrance – with contemporary racism and the necessity to create an inclusive French citizenship.[142] Moreover, the parliamentary debate – and the coverage the 23 February law then received in the media for months – became the first sustained political public engagement with colonial history in France and in Europe.

Seeking a way out of the political impasse, President Chirac rescinded the law in January 2006 after calling it a 'great fuckup'.[143] However, by that time the issue of how to remember the colonial past had become a marker of political identity. Left-wing politicians, activists and intellectuals adopted the need of autocritical approach to colonial history as an identification of the left, while right-wing deputies and intellectuals, mostly rallied behind the then minister of interior and later president Nicolas Sarkozy, articulated a politics of 'no repentance' as a reply to debates about colonial history.[144] For Stora, who had previously called on French society to face its colonial past for the sake of 'healing', the acrimony was a sign that these debates had gone too far and created a 'surfeit of memory'.[145] The historian defined the new state of debate over colonial history as 'memory wars', in which different representatives of minority groups had weaponised the Duty to remember in a 'competition of victimhood' that opened up more wounds than it healed. Simultaneously, however, while these so-called memory wars reflected that the politicisation

---

[141] Lotem, *The Memory of Colonialism in Britain and France*, pp. 124–28 and Bertrad, *Mémoires d'empire*.

[142] Lotem, *The Memory of Colonialism in Britain and France*, pp. 160–67.

[143] *Le Monde*, 18 October 2005.

[144] Lotem, *The Memory of Colonialism in Britain and France*, pp. 177–86.

[145] Stora, *Les guerres sans fin, un historien entre la France et l'Algérie*.

of memory was not a tool to heal society's wounds, the contestation of history opened up avenues for different actors to call on the state to address their grievances and take minority voices into account.

The year 2005 was marked not only by governmental debates but also the emergence of a new generation of antiracist organisations, whether the radical *Mouvement des Indigènes de République* (MIR) and the *Brigade anti-négrophobie* (BAN), or the moderate and institutionalised *Conseil représentatif des associations noires* (Representative Council of Black Associations, CRAN). Despite different trajectories, founding members of all these associations stated that the reason for their gestation was the necessity to openly address the racial element that defined their existence as non-white, racialised subjects in the French republic.[146] In the French context, this statement was not innocuous. The French republican model perceived the French state as 'one and indivisible' and colour blind. The republic, accordingly, cannot treat any of its citizens differently, as this would amount to unrepublican discrimination, and thus could not acknowledge any specificities (or specific demands) of any minority communities, as this would constitute '*communautarisme*', or community separatism.[147] The very use of the word race was problematic at best, as popular and political discourse still linked it to biological race theories of the ninteenth century and European fascism. Without addressing the social structures and categorisation of race in a state that was 'colour blind', activists realised that it became impossible to address systemic racism. To find a way out of this contradiction, all these very different organisations turned to the debate on colonial history and memory, which gave them a vocabulary to address race. Through reading of francophone anticolonial theories like Aimé Césaire's and Frantz Fanon's, but also English language postcolonial texts, these new organisations articulated the necessity to address French colonial continuities to explain and fight contemporary racism. The most memorable linking between colonial history and contemporary racism remained the MIR's founding document from January 2005. It denounced housing and employment discrimination of non-white citizens, which the MIR called 'indigenised population' as a reference to the colonial status of indigenous subjects as it claimed that 'France remains a colonial state'.[148] For the MIR, but also the other organisations, 'colonial continuities' became a lens through which to analyse contemporary racism and discrimination.

None of these new antiracist organisations was primarily interested in the Duty to remember or the memorial mechanisms that it addressed. The very

---

[146] Lotem, 'Anti-racist Activism and the Memory of Colonialism', pp. 283–98.

[147] On concepts of *communautarisme*, see Chabal, *A Divided Republic*.

[148] Mouvement the Indigènes de la République, *Appel des Indigènes de la République*.

memorial debates, state recognition or the erection of memorials were second-ary to their goals of addressing systemic discrimination. However, the avail-ability of vocabulary of autocritical memory allowed them to address the very position of racialised subjects in France and establish a discursive link between colonial history and racialisation in the present. One such example is the case of the CRAN's decision in 2012 to demand reparation for slavery from French banks and financial institutions that had profited from the enslavement of Africans for the sake of using reparation money for contemporary Black communities in France.[149] In so doing, the organisation tied the politics of memory to the very definition of French Blackness, which had been absent from Caribbean activism's memory activism in the 1990s. By the 2010s, the linking of colonial memory to 'race' had become a constitutive element of French antiracism, as yet a newer generation of activist organisations emerged, which focused ever more on addressing 'race' as an antiracist strategy. For Afrofeminist organisations like Mwasi or the popular activist and journalist Rokhaya Diallo, demanding to 'talk about race' through acknowledgement of colonial history became the main goal of antiracist action.[150]

The trajectory of French memory debates reflects the potential of Duty to remember to incite broader memory debates. The very principle of Duty to remember emerged from the specific context of the Holocaust, and the inability to keep silent facing the growing recognition of the moral importance of dealing with the Holocaust as a crime on the level of the French state. Nonetheless, the availability of the model for other communities in France opened up new avenues of defining minority groups' belonging in a postcolonial state. For Caribbean movements demanding recognition as citizens, historians demand-ing engagement with the Algerian War of Independence or antiracist activists interested in race, the political rationale of memory became a tool for addressing the responsibility of the French state.

Memory debates emerged from the assumption that autocritical memory – or the facing of the past – would result in 'healing'. The outcomes of more autocritical debate, however, were nowhere close to appeasing, as acrimonious memory debates became a battleground of their own. Actors of all political convictions appropriated memory to make demands of state in society alike and mobilised memory as a battleground. This demonstrated the potential of auto-critical memory to absorb new issues and incite new debates. The French case was particularly fruitful for this kind of development due to the tradition of French antiracist activists to centre their demands on the state. By calling on the

---

[149] Lotem, 'Anti-racist Activism and the Memory of Colonialism', p. 296.
[150] Lotem, *The Memory of Colonialism in Britain and France*, pp. 155–57.

state to address historical wrongdoings, they continued autocritical debates about ways to reinvent a collective postcolonial French identity. Similarly, while the politicisation of colonial memory in France addressed French responsibility for French crimes that were global in nature, debates in France remained focused on the French nation, whether through focus on national belonging or the models of the French state. This explains the different timeline of French colonial memory debates as opposed to elsewhere in Europe, as these emerged from a longer continuity of memorial contestation. The next section returns to Germany, another national case of autocritical memory, where the mobilisation of the autocritical model of *Vergangenheitsbewältigung* to address colonial history and racism occurred in reaction to more global dynamics and cues.

3.2 *Vergangenheitsbewältigung* in Multi-ethnic Germany: What to Do with Germany's Colonial Past?

This section explores the transformations of memory debates in Germany in the 2000s, as different actors began questioning the usefulness of Germany's memory culture, represented by the now ubiquitous political rationale of *Vergangenheitsbewältigung* (see Section 1). As the reunited Federal Republic became a European multi-ethnic state despite the intentions of West German governments' citizenship policies, intellectuals and antiracist activists called on state and society to rearticulate German identity to fit with its new realities. In this process, public debates increasingly focused on the supposed 'success' of Germany's memory culture in creating a more inclusive identity and to fight racism. To do so, they borrowed from global debates about colonialism and race to demand greater visibility of German colonial history in Germany's memory culture, but also raised the question of whether German remembrance was fit for purpose in the twenty-first century.

3.2.1 Memory Culture in a Diverse Germany

The first crises of Germany's so-called memory culture occurred in the 1990s, through debates about the role of autocritical memory in a united Germany and in a diverse 'immigration society'. While autocritical memory had turned into a marker of identity and socialisation in West Germany, the reinvention of German society in the years after reunification and in the 2000s showed that the specific West German debates of the post-war periods were not as easily transposable onto a diverse society. In both cases, the need to reinvent new narratives that included either citizens socialised in the former GDR or 'new Germans' whose ancestors did not bear any personal responsibility for Nazi crimes posed a challenge to the recent unifying consensus of West German autocritical identity as a marker of renewal and progress.

Firstly, as German reunification after 1990 resulted in the 'integration' of the former East into the much larger West German state, West German authorities harnessed the logic of *Vergangenheitsbewältigung* to address the East German dictatorship. Cleaning up East Germany included the purging of institutions – like universities – and replacing East German officials with West German ones. In the same 'truth telling' logic of the Argentinian model, the government appointed a committee to 'work through' the dictatorship, which resulted in making Stasi documents available to the public to reveal the extent of East German surveillance and oppression mechanisms and the creation of new museums and memorials to address these.[151] New German governments mobilised the notion of autocritical memory as a way to 'heal' East German society, but in so doing imposed a model of remembrance as a part of what many East Germans perceived as a West German takeover. Just as importantly, the autocritical model of 'dealing' with the Holocaust became a subject of many debates about the integration of the former GDR. Here again, new governments imposed a model that had emerged through West German debates on responsibility to 'integrate' East Germans. In the GDR, rejection of the fascist past had been a part of the Socialist state's legitimating discourse. Nonetheless, this same discourse had not accepted continuities with the Nazi regimes, but claimed complete rupture, while painting the capitalist Federal Republic as the natural successor of fascism and the home of Nazi perpetrators.[152] The imposition of West German autocritical memory of dealing with Nazi crimes as a defining characteristic of German identity thus resulted in tensions about the 'compatibility' of East German political socialisation with the model of autocritical remembrance.

Secondly, the transformation of Germany into a multi-ethnic postcolonial state contributed to new tensions about the adequacy of the country's memory culture in an ever-changing landscape. In the 1990s, political debates about 'immigration' and 'integration' became increasingly visible, most notably about the place of non-European immigrants who had arrived in the period of the so-called economic miracle, in large numbers from Turkey.[153] The first generation arrived as 'guest workers'. The category reflected West German authorities' lack of desire for immigrants to stay and the lack of legal framework for 'guests' to become German citizens. Two generations later, 'new Germans'

---

[151] See, for example, Miller, *The Stasi Files Unveiled*.   [152] Herf, *Divided Memory*.

[153] On immigration history to Germany, see, for example, Hans, 'Deutschland als Einwanderungsland', pp. 25–42, and Schönwälder, 'Migration und Ausländerpolitik in der Bundesrepublik Deutschland Öffentliche Debatten und politische Entscheidungen', pp. 106–19.

were born into a country in which they were not citizens and had no political discourse to articulate their belonging. As political debates focused on the 'failed integration' of these immigrants, the political conversation revolved around the question of whether German society needed to accept it was a 'society of immigration'. In the 2000s, a growing number of mainly left-wing actors demanded to accept diversity as a self-evident reality of the country. In the same vein, they called on state and society to change legislation and rearticulate German identity to include 'new Germans'.[154]

A German specialty, however, was the role of autocritical memory in the articulation of German identity. Here, one recurrent theme that marked debates about immigration from an early stage was the supposed rejection of German memory culture by Muslim 'immigrants'. Citing evidence from schools with a large proportion of children of Turkish, Lebanese and Palestinian origin, media reports suggested that antisemitism of immigrant communities had passed onto children, who rejected Holocaust education as not relevant to their family histories.[155] In these debates, remembrance of the Holocaust reflected an inherent element of a new German identity, where 'being German' meant engaging with the legacy of Nazi crimes. For a broad spectrum of German actors, its rejection represented a refusal to join a German community defined by the 'progress' of dealing with the past. Moreover, many of the reports about rejection of responsibility for Nazi crimes focused on children's animosity towards the State of Israel in the context of the Israeli–Arab conflict. Different commentators were therefore confronted with another principle of *Vergangenheitsbewältigung*. While absent from the first decades of such debates, by the early 2000s, a political consensus had emerged among large parts of the German political elite that the German state held a specific responsibility for the existence of the world's only Jewish state.[156]

In the late 2000s, growing pedagogical literature about 'dealing with the past in an immigration society' reflected a new contradiction for left-wing actors.[157] On the one hand, autocritical memory had shaped identities on the left about German responsibility. On the other hand, the inclusion of 'new Germans' whose families did not share any personal responsibilities for Nazi crimes required rearticulation of German identity, or at the very least adaption of the rationale of autocritical memory to address a more abstract German identity rather than one that relied on interrogation of one's own family's heritage. These works often focused on the necessity to adapt Germany's memory culture as an

---

[154] See, for example, Foroutan, 'Neue Deutsche, Postmigranten und Bindungs-Identitäten'.

[155] Georgi, Kahle, Freund and Wiezorek, 'Perspektiven von Lehrkräften', pp. 61–123.

[156] See, for example, Möller, Grote, Nolde and Schumacher, *'Die kann ich nicht ab!'*.

[157] See, for example, Messerschmidt, 'Geschichtsbewusstsein ohne Identitätsbesetzungen', pp. 16–22 and Baader and Freytag (eds.), *Erinnerungskulturen*.

abstract good that increasingly focused on the values of antiracism and 'never again' to appeal to children who found the specific focus on Nazi family connections unrelatable, or even politically objectionable in the light of support for the Palestinian cause. Simultaneously, however, 'new Germans' of different origins, whose voices were often absent from debates about 'integration', began questioning the very adequacy of Germany's memory culture in a postcolonial Germany. For them, memory needed to be less 'German' and more globalised. They demanded German society to mobilise its much vaunted memory culture to fight racism and address Germany's colonial history.

3.2.2 Challenging a 'Parochial' Memory Culture for the Sake of 'Globality'

German debates about the country's past had rarely focused on the country's relatively short colonial history. Between the 1880s and the First World War, the German empire subjugated various territories in Africa and the Pacific, which the Chancellor Otto von Bismarck defined as protectorates, and became the world's third largest colonial empire. After the loss in the First World War, the new German government was forced to cede all its imperial possessions to the victors. While colonial continuities still defined German military and political culture in the aftermath of the First World War, the lack of broad personal contacts with colonial territories help explain the lack of references to colonial history. Moreover, as immigration to Germany did not occur from its former colonies, racialised minorities in Germany did not address continuities with colonial oppression to address contemporary racism and demand equal rights as postcolonial citizens, as was the case in France. Here, few to no communities in Germany transmitted narratives about their own connections to German overseas empires, neither through continuities with colonial armies nor as victims. Nonetheless, to observers and historians, the inclusion of German colonial history into its autocritical memory culture made sense in the abstract as a chapter that required acknowledging and addressing. Simultaneously, however, it lacked the immediate visibility through personal connections and popular myths. While the necessity of addressing Nazi crimes in the 1950s made sense to audiences within immediate and living memory of these, prioritising engagement with older colonial crimes was not self-evident.

One aspect of German colonial history that returned to haunt the country's 'memory culture' a century later was the genocide of the Herrero and Nama people in German Southwest Africa (today Namibia) between 1904 and 1908.[158] The German military's massacre of tens of thousands of Herreros and Namas following an anti-colonial revolt became increasingly acknowledged as the first

---

[158] See, for example, Zimmerer and Zeller (eds.), *Völkermord in Deutsch-Südwestafrika*.

genocide of the twentieth century. This engagement occurred in both academic works like Hannah Arendt's Origins of Totalitarianism and in more official instances the case of the UN Human Rights Commission's *Whitaker Report* from 1983.[159] Moreover, Herrero and Nama groups long demanded an official apology and reparations from Germany. For a long time, these demands were met with German silence, which was best embodied by the German Chancellor Helmut Kohl's refusal to meet Herrero representatives during his visit in 1995, the first state visit of a German Chancellor to Namibia. In the early 2000s, however, increased Herrero pressure through unsuccessful lawsuits forced German governments to engage with the history of the genocide. For example, in 2004, the Minister of Development Heidemarie Wieczorek-Zeul attended the commemorations of the genocide's centenary in Namibia. She expressed her deepest regret while ruling out financial reparations beyond extended development aid.[160] This reflected the dynamics in which different German official actors would reluctantly be forced to make statements, also through Herrero and Namibian demands, but insist that moral acknowledgement should suffice rather than financial reparations.

The Herrero and Nama genocide was an event that could be harnessed as an example for the violence of German colonialism and as a precursor to Nazi crimes. Despite its low visibility in the German public conversation, it represented a bone of contention in German foreign relations with Namibia. It was not until the 2010s, however, that German actors chose to focus on the necessity to 'come to terms' with German colonial crimes. Just like in France, they did so through demands to live up to German autocritical standards and include colonial history in German 'memory culture' to shape a truly progressive German society, as changes in Germany in the 2000s required a new rearticulation of German identities. Unlike the French case, however, these actors' choice to focus on colonial history did not draw on national references but took inspiration from global debates and called on German society to become more cosmopolitan. These debates were led by historians and antiracist activists who challenged the 'parochial' and closed nature of German debates. Simultaneously, conservative actors, who had previously resisted 'coming to terms' with Nazi crimes, had taken to defending German 'memory culture' and the primacy of the Holocaust within it as an inherently German phenomenon.

---

[159] See Arendt, *The Origins of Totalitarianism*.

[160] On memory politics and the role of the genocide in relations between Germany and Namibia, see Kößler and Melber, *Völkermord – und was dann? Die Politik deutsch-namibischer Vergangenheitsbearbeitung* and Kößler, *Namibia and Germany*.

One of the people who became most identified with demands to address Germany's colonial history was the global historian Jürgen Zimmerer, who became the University of Hamburg's chair for global history in 2010 after an international academic career. For Zimmerer, German uninterest in engaging with the history of the Herrero and Nama genocide reflected a crack in the edifice of Germany's autocritical memory. Just as importantly, however, it was also a sign of German lack of interest in global debates that were increasingly turning towards global interpretative paradigms and decolonial histories. He condemned not only the lack of official recognition of the genocide but also the lack of incorporation of this genocide into Germany's broader 'memory culture'. In so doing, he was not different from Benjamin Stora in France, whose early life mission was to get the French to care about their colonial past and particularly the Algerian War of Independence. Zimmerer, however, came from a different position, as he was initially far more invested in academic debates than public conversations. His initial interventions on the continuities between the Herrero genocide and the Holocaust mainly remained on the pages of academic journals.[161] At the University of Hamburg, he created an academic community focused on colonial continuities in Germany, most notably about the colonial significance – and colonial legacies – of Hamburg, Europe's once largest port.[162] Here, Zimmerer used his opportunity to enter the public sphere in 2015 with the debate about the (re)construction of Berlin's palace that came to house the controversial ethnographic museum of the Humboldt Forum.

The Berlin palace had been a symbol for the changing face of the city and the relationship between memory and the built environment. In 1950, the East German authorities demolished the previous residence of Prussian Kings as a symbol of Prussian militarism. After reunification, the authorities of the Federal Republic decided to remove the Palace of the Republic built in its stead as a symbol of the SED dictatorship.[163] However, the demolition of the Palace of the Republic was designed to make space for the reconstruction of that same symbol of Prussian militarism following a conservative fundraising campaign in the 1990s that had raised over 120 million EUR in private donations. To soften the problematic connotations of rebuilding a Prussian palace, the Bundestag decided to use the space of the reconstructed palace as a 'universalist' cultural space that would house collections of the Berlin's 'world' museums, the Ethnological Museum and a Museum for Asian Art. The new museum was opened in July 2021. For critics of the project, the decision of using the

---

[161] See Zimmerer's monograph *Von Windhuk nach Auschwitz?* but also for example, 'Die Geburt des "Ostlandes" aus dem Geiste des Kolonialismus', pp. 10–43.

[162] The main publication to date from the Hamburg project is Todzi and Zimmerer, *Hamburg*.

[163] Brusius, 'Das Humboldtforum ist nur der Anfang'.

reconstructed palace space to house objects of colonial provenance symbolised Germany's postcolonial malaise more than anything else. The country's pride in its 'memory culture' stood in stark contrast to the absence of remembrance of colonialism, in particular in museums that were facing reckoning with their colonial collections worldwide. Thus, 'the world was watching' Germany's 'silence', which required an 'open debate of civil society(ies) [...] about the meaning of the global historical phenomenon of colonialism for Germany'.[164] Zimmerer contrasted Germany's national memory culture, which he often characterised as parochial, with a necessity to become attuned to global debates. He used an available political memory vocabulary that assumed the importance of memory for German society in demanding German identity become more global in nature.

The same logic became even more apparent a few years later, in summer 2020, with the so-called Mbembe debate about antisemitism as postcolonialism, which refocused attention on the meaning of German memory culture for Germany and beyond. In May 2020, the government's Antisemitism Commissioner Felix Klein demanded the Cameroonian postcolonial intellectual Achille Mbembe, who was supposed to open the art festival Ruhrtriennale (which was later cancelled because of the coronavirus pandemic), be disinvited. Klein argued that the intellectual had engaged in 'relativisation of the Holocaust' and criticism of Israel, particularly through comparisons with Apartheid in South Africa.[165] In so doing, he linked Mbembe to a new political debate in Germany, where right-wing politicians had demanded to outlaw the international anti-Zionist Boycott, Divestment and Sanctions movement (BDS) on grounds that it was antisemitic and thus incompatible with Germany's memory culture and inherent responsibility for the existence of the world's only Jewish state.[166] Mbembe, who quickly claimed he had 'no relation to BDS' and had never relativised the Holocaust despite criticism of Israel, became a symbol for a wider debate about the relations between anti-Zionism and antisemitism.

While this debate was international and raged in many other countries,[167] in Germany it quickly focused on the country's memory culture and its role in the twenty-first century. On the one hand, conservative politicians and intellectuals returned to Germany's specific responsibility to fighting antisemitism, which they equated with supporting the State of Israel, and condemned demands to

---

[164] Zimmerer, 'Der Kolonialismus ist kein Spiel'.

[165] *Frankfurter Allgemeine Zeitung*, 8 June 2020.

[166] See, for example, *Berliner Zeitung*, 22 December 2020.

[167] See, for example, the debate in France, where the National assembly continuously debates resolutions about BDS and anti-Zionism, see, for example, *Le Monde*, 2 December 2019.

address the country's colonial past next to the Holocaust as 'relativisation' of the Holocaust. On the other hand, a growing number of observers, whether 700 international intellectuals who signed a letter of support of Mbembe,[168] international historians of Germany or antiracist activists in Germany, argued that the narrow focus of 'memory culture' on the Holocaust and support of Israel was not fit for purpose in the twenty-first century. Not only did it serve as a way of ignoring crimes committed by the Israeli state and military but it also reflected a German identity that was no longer relevant in the 2020s.

The engagement of international scholars with the German memory debate became ever more visible consequently, as the Australian genocide scholar Dirk Moses published an article called 'The Catechism of Germans' in May 2021.[169] Moses mocked German attachment to the singularity of Holocaust memory as parochial and reactionary. While international scholars like the American memory scholar Michael Rothberg and Jürgen Zimmerer had been discussing links between colonialism and the Holocaust for two decades, Moses claimed, German elites were stuck in a parochial, national mindset. They had adopted the Holocaust's singularity as a 'catechism', or an element of religious belief, which they defended against 'heresy' of those who wish to challenge it by integrating perspectives of other victims into the German narrative. In so doing, they instrumentalise the Holocaust to hide other crimes and exclude the narratives of 'new Germans'. According to Moses, German elites therefore needed to abandon their memorial catechism and create a new memory culture through broader inspiration from global decolonial movements.

The article triggered a debate that was first limited to international scholars of Germany online, but quickly expanded into German media to include often enraged reactions by German historians and intellectuals.[170] Firstly, some objected to the claim that, in the German case at the very least, the Holocaust's specificity could not be understood without including colonial history. Secondly, the sarcastic tone of the article, in which a non-German made demands of German national identity, enraged German scholars further. Nonetheless, the debate reflected a globalisation of the conversation about memory in Germany. International interest in German memory was not by any means new, as the

---

[168] For further commentary on the debate, see Capdepón and Moses (eds.), 'Forum', pp. 371–77.

[169] Moses, 'Der Katechismus der Deutschen'.

[170] The most sustained debate following Moses' publication was curated by the Canadian historian Jennifer Evans under the online on the platform NewFascismSyllabus: http://newfascismsyllabus .com/wp-content/uploads/2021/08/The-Catechism-Debate.pdf (last accessed on 23 February 2023), but see also reactions in the German media, for example *Berliner Zeitung*, 11 August 2021 and 30 August 2021, where the culture editor Hanno Hauenstein sought out various specialist voices to comment the debate. See also *Frankfurter Allgemeine Zeitung*, 31 August 2021.

German 'success story' had been often debated in the world.[171] The novelty in this debate was international observers' disappointment with the German model's failure to live up to what they considered was its promise of creating a more inclusive society. Online reactions to Moses included many international observers of Germany and non-Germans living in Germany, who published many English language reactions, mostly in support of Moses' thesis and tone. Beyond support of the need to reform German memory culture through engagement with histories of other victims, reactions by international scholars reflected resentment of the same 'parochial' and navel-gazing nature that Moses mocked.[172] What observers resented the most was the pride German actors took in the country's national memory culture. They argued that arrogant belief in the moral superiority of German memory culture had made the latter exclusionary to the voices of 'new Germans' with their connection to global histories of oppression and German exclusion through colonial racism.

Simultaneously, new antiracist voices in Germany had also begun demanding an overhaul of the country's memory culture for the sake of fighting racism and creating a more inclusive Germanness. These antiracist 'public' activists had all come from different traditions and groupings of German antiracist movements, from Afro-German movements of the 1980s that drew their inspiration from African American writing,[173] 'self-defence' groups like Antifaşist Gençlik[174] or Antifa organisations that arose in protest after recurrent far-right violence.[175] In the 2010s, a new generation of antiracist activists became increasingly visible in the public sphere with demands to be included in a German narrative that reflected a diverse German society – and their own place in it as equal citizens with hyphenated identities. In a growing number of publications,[176] authors demanded to challenge the German narrative of 'integration' that forced minorities to integrate into a German white majority society. In so doing, one symbol for the rigidity of German identity was the German memory narrative that demanded autocritical thinking from people whose own families had not shared any responsibility for Nazi crimes but had suffered from colonial oppression and postcolonial racism in Germany. These activists were connected to antiracist debates around the world and drew their inspiration from the Black Lives Matter movement in the US and recurrent debates elsewhere in Europe about

---

[171] For one of the latest such conversations, see Susan Neiman's intervention in the US debate, Neiman, *Learning from the Germans*.

[172] Neiman, *Learning from the Germans*.   [173] Florvil, *Mobilizing Black Germany*.

[174] Özcan, *Türkische Immigrantenorganisationen in der Bundesrepublik Deutschland*.

[175] Kahveci, 'Transversale Politik des Antirassismus und Antifaschismus?', pp. 219–32.

[176] See, for example, Czollek, *Desintegriert euch!*

the need to address racism through understanding of colonial history. In so doing, they appropriated the demand to reform the country's 'memory culture' as means to address the challenge of fighting racism in the present. One such example is the book *Eure Heimat ist unser Albtraum* (your 'home' is our nightmare, 2021),[177] in which a group of intersectional and antiracist voices published various texts about the different facets of otherness in Germany. In various accounts of daily humiliations of members of different communities, one recurrent argument was that 'being 'home' means being a part of its memory culture'.[178] Racial justice in Germany, then, implied changing the country's memory culture, where the supposed 'success' of autocritical reflection had made way for a new brand of German nationalism. The co-optation of a previously revolutionary autocritical demands by German conservative actors who wished to retain the status quo and block voices of new racialised citizens became the new target of German antiracist activists. In other words, as previously transformative autocritical memory had turned into a self-congratulatory mechanism of the German state, its shortcomings became ever more visible.

The one thing missing from demands of scholars and antiracist activists to 'reform' German memory culture was, however, an acknowledgement of what memory could – and could not – achieve, and particularly Germany's autocritical model. In line with growing global attention to memory as a victim-centred tool for fighting racism, a growing number of actors began addressing the German model as one that had been invented to fight antisemitism after the Holocaust rather than the result of an inner-German (and particularly West German) debate that focused solely on the identity of descendants of perpetrators. The specific power of the German model was also associated to the immediacy of confronting one's family past in a place where nearly every family had a past to confront. The establishment of German memory culture assumed a shared responsibility, but responsibility as an abstract concept was complemented by rituals that reminded Germans that autocriticism meant digging into their own family histories. Demands to recentre Germany's memory culture on colonial history sought to re-establish memory as an abstract concept that defined German responsibility without the immediacy of family continuities. To compensate for the lack of immediate family history, these calls fostered a sense of cosmopolitanism, as German actors would be following worldly cues and conversations. In so doing, however, the very German focus became contradictory: on the one hand, actors calling to reform German

---

[177] Aydemir and Yaghoobifarah (eds.), *Eure Heimat ist unser Albtraum.*

[178] Aydemir and Yaghoobifarah (eds.), *Eure Heimat ist unser Albtraum*, p. 117.

memory culture depicted memory as the all-powerful key to fight racism and transform German society. On the other hand, however, through viewing of German memory ahistorically and through the lens of victim-based global conversations, they failed to address the thing that had made it so powerful in the first place: the autocritical component.

In fact, the German political trajectory reflected the demise of autocritical thinking, just as a global conversation about colonial history was emerging. While the German memory 'model' had inspired international actors in the 1990s, new social movements in the late 2010s followed cues from the US and the Global South. In the febrile crisis-laden atmosphere of the 2010s, new generations of activists and intellectuals embraced a focus on the past as means of resistance and fighting racism.[179] From the Rhodes Must Fall protests in Cape Town in 2015 and later in Oxford to the contestation of the equestrian statue of Robert E. Lee in Richmond, Virginia, in 2017, new antiracist coalitions and movements targeted symbols of past colonial domination and white supremacy. They did so to address the salience of racism in present-day society against the backdrop of a global rise of the far-right.[180] Simultaneously, new bestselling works by Black and racialised intellectuals from Reni Eddo-Lodge to Akala, Rokhaya Diallo or Mohmamed Amjahid, increasingly addressed race in Europe's and North America's multiracial democracies.[181] In these instances, activists and intellectuals insisted on the novelty of 'making history'[182] through toppling statues as reckoning with 'forgotten' colonial history. The claim of novelty placed these new contestations outside existing conversations about 'memory'. While these contestations were memory politics at its very basic form, the activists, intellectuals, journalists and politicians in these anglophone conversations did not use the word 'memory' to refer to what was going on. In so doing, anglophone memory activists did not consider themselves within the continuity of a trajectory of memorial contestation shaped by autocritical memory. Their goals were more ambitious than focusing on narratives. Topping statues and cleaning up public spaces intended to be an active tool in

---

[179]　While memory activism has always had a clear relation to contestation of narratives of the status quo, the 2010s saw a growth of a more explicit use of resistance as a way to mobilising support for the re-examination of the past, see, for example, Gopal, *Insurgent Empire*.

[180]　On the context of Unite the Right in the US, see the *Washington Post*, 8 September 2021 on the removal of the statue. On protests see the *New York Times*, 20 November 2017. Otherwise see Fall, *Rhodes Must Fall*. See also Lotem, *The Memory of Colonialism in Britain and France*, pp. 315–19.

[181]　See, for example, Eddo-Lodge, *Why I'm No Longer Talking to White People about Race*, Akala, *Natives*, Hirsch, *Brit(ish)*, and Olusoga, *Black and British*, but also Diallo, *La France* and Amjahid, *Der weiße Fleck*.

[182]　See, for example, Olusoga, 'The Toppling of Edward Colston's Statue Is Not an Attack on History'.

the fight against racism, as removing traces of racist pasts would create inclusive spaces for racialised minorities.[183]

The idea that contesting the past was a revolutionary novelty rather than a continuity that borrowed from other 'models' affected memory actors' ability to articulate and achieve their goals. In places that had no tradition of autocritical memory, like the UK, the lack of any 'memory vocabulary' that identified memory as a political rationale in its own right made it harder for a public debate to move beyond a 'balance sheet' logic, in which different memory actors continuously debated whether colonialism had simply been 'good' or 'bad'.[184] Conservative and antiracist actors co-opted the debate about colonial history into a culture war logic, but without the horizon that explained why British society as a whole needed to address issues of responsibility or introspection. Similarly, with any lack of common consensus about what memory was for beyond political acrimony, it became harder to articulate what 'dealing with the past' could mean in practice.

In Germany or France, the existence of an autocritical memory rationale made it easier for activists to mobilise colonial history alongside other histories and initiate a public conversation about its meaning in public and create new public spaces dedicated to colonial history. Even here, however, these debates were not 'appeased', just as earlier debates about the memory of the Holocaust had been full of acrimony. The existing rationale only helped activists find the words to establish their goals as relevant for a broad political conversation – but also attracted the ire of conservative actors. Simultaneously, debates in Europe reflected the centrality of anglophone ideas and vocabulary, as they followed developments from the US and the Global South. In so doing, German activists, for example, focused their attention on attacking what they perceived as a reactionary German memory culture rather than borrowing from its strengths. Doing the latter would have required a more historical understanding of *Vergangenheitsbewältigung*'s emergence as an autocritical principle before its development into a political rationale of the German state.

3.3 Conclusion

As European postcolonial societies struggled to redefine themselves and articulate new and inclusive identities for citizens with origins in the Global South, memory became a battleground for new debates. It allowed politicians and activists to articulate new identities in battles about race and national identity

---

[183] See, for example, Younge, 'Why Every Statue Should Come Down'.

[184] On the 'Balance Sheet' concept, see Lotem, *The Memory of Colonialism in Britain and France*, pp. 364–72.

(not least by questioning the place of European identities in an increasingly globalised and Americanised world). The near-simultaneous perfect storm of debates about memory in nearly all Western European polities – with different colonial and postcolonial trajectories – demonstrated the strength of circulation of ideas about memory in Europe and beyond. Everywhere in Europe, academics and antiracist activists turned to memory to explain colonial continuities into the present in a moment of democratic crisis, a rising far-right and necessity to articulate the sense of multi-ethnic European societies. After debates about 'immigration' and multiculturalism in the 1990s, the rise of visible Islamophobia in the early 2000s after the US's so-called War on Terror and through the rise of inequalities after the global economic crisis of 2008, antiracist actors in Europe searched for a new language to explain the role of race and salience of racism in European societies. Colonial history and existing memory models, whether through successful autocritical models, the rise of what Lea David calls 'moral remembrance', or Natan Sznaider's rationale of 'never again', provided a vocabulary to address frustration with the long-standing exclusion of racialised minorities in democratic polities. These actors borrowed from exiting memory rationales as well as from global conversations about race, resistance and activism.

Autocritical memory was particularly important in the gestation of these debates. In countries that had already established a political rationale of autocritical memory as a defining element of national identities that had been reinvented after the Second World War, like France and Germany, this political rationale offered inroads for antiracist activists to demand another reinvention. Actors in France and Germany called on the political elite and society to address histories of colonial oppression to explain the connection between postcolonial immigrants and their home societies, and create more 'inclusive' identities.

Antiracist activists expanded the autocritical imperative to include colonial history through challenging existing rationales as oppressive, but also as failures to fight against racism. They borrowed much more from two decades of global debates about moral remembrance than from national trajectories where autocritical debates had emerged. If *Vergangenheitsbewältigung* emerged from the very immediate continuity with family history and responsibility, claiming that it can be harnessed as an abstract common good to fight racism required a reinterpretation of memory as a universalist moral imperative. This, however, also points out to the limits of memory. If the use of autocritical memory was helpful in opening up new debates about the present, there is no evidence for how remembering the past can fix these same issues.

Conclusion

This Element has followed the gestation of 'memory politics' as we know it today. The emergence of autocritical memory in West Germany created a new political rationale that identified German transformation with commemorating and 'dealing' with Nazi crimes. It created a new understanding of memory that prioritised engagement with a polity's dark history rather than past glory or glorious sacrifices. Its success has created new understandings of memory, yet as new demands emerged to 'heal' societies through engagement with their pasts, the specificities of autocritical memory have been lost. In other words, this is a story of the rise and fall of autocritical memory. Understanding it requires attention to why the initial West German articulation of memory 'succeeded' and how the international borrowing transformed the German historical specificities into an abstract model that could not meet moral expectations international actors identified with 'dealing with the past'.

The articulation of national autocritical memory rationales in West Germany and France after the war transpired over lengthy processes of articulation of ideas by intellectuals and their adoption by political and cultural elites. These processes spanned several generations and ended in the establishment of 'responsibility' for past crimes as a defining feature of either polity. In both cases, intellectuals and politicians addressed autocritical memory as a national endeavour to reinvent societies through acknowledging direct continuities between crimes of the Second World War and post-war states, but without a dialogue with victims. In other words, they identified recognition of responsibility with a future-oriented transformation. Particularly in the German case, this long-term acceptance of an autocritical model was intertwined with a necessity to legitimise a post-war democracy that distanced itself credibly – for its own sake and in the eyes of the world – from the crimes of its predecessors. Intellectuals who addressed these crimes did so through accepting their scale and the implication of most citizens in them. The so-called success of *Vergangenheitsbewältigung*, which became identified with the peaceful democratisation of West Germany, set the stage for the contemporary identification of memory with the 'healing' of societies. Simultaneously, the globalisation of Holocaust memory and the growth of international remembrance of the victims of the Holocaust raised the problematic impression of a 'successful' global memory trend that provided justice for victims. Between the global dimension of Holocaust remembrance and the very national 'success' of German memory culture, international actors and activists sought to draw on memory's potential in articulating best-practice models to be implemented in new cases of democratisation at the end of the third wave of democratisation. Following on examples of 'successful' memory, international actors viewed memory as an abstract good that could be shaped into a proper kind of remembrance through often abstract repetition of moral principles of 'never again' and focus on victims' testimonies. Many actors were able to mobilise this rationale for the formulation of political demands as European societies faced challenges to their post-war settlements, and required to explain this decline through long-term continuities. The ahistorical, moral and abstract understanding of memory, however, voided it of the specificity that underpinned cases of 'successful' transformation in the post-war era.

The international circulation of a 'model' of so-called moral remembrance, to paraphrase Lea David, contributed to the development of what seemed like a common frame of references for global actors. The different case studies in the Element, however, show how different actors mobilised new understandings of memory for different purposes in vastly different contexts. The rise of memory was therefore not a homogenous phenomenon, but an uneven process that shifted through the understandings of various actors – not least academics and activists. Starting with international actors' desire to harness Germany's memorial 'success' to force reconciliation between (descendants of) perpetrators and victims, activists and academics began focusing on the past to demand ending inequalities. In so doing, they appropriated autocritical memory as a tool to increase empathy for victims, ignoring the very imperfect essence of the development of autocritical memory: victims had been all but absent from German memorial debates. Dealing with the past thus developed into a tool for victims to demand their own place in national narratives, but with moral expectations that could not be met.

The theorisation of memory from its autocritical source into a 'model' ignored another characteristic that underpinned its German success, which was memory politics' connection to material conditions. In fact, the acceptance of the autocritical 'model' in West Germany occurred in a time of economic growth and necessity to legitimise a new German democracy in a period of future-oriented reinvention. The transformation of West German society was the result of many material aspects that were intertwined with acceptance of responsibility. Memory was, in other words, just one element of West Germany's unexpected transformation into a peaceful liberal democracy. Nonetheless, German transformation and establishment of autocritical identity did not do away with antisemitism and racism, which became ever more pronounced in later periods of crisis. This shows that memory itself is not enough to fight racism and inequalities. Antiracist actors in the present day are therefore faced with a dilemma. On the one hand, the vocabulary of memory has been helpful in critiquing state and society alike. Addressing colonial continuities has become a strong explanatory tool that addressed the salience of race in contemporary societies. On the other hand, the moral expectations invested in commemoration, language and discourse cannot be met without attention to the material conditions that shape society.

Ultimately, however, this Element's focus on autocritical memory wishes to draw attention to the value in autocritical remembrance. While 'dealing with the past' cannot solve the present, it can lead to more truthful public narratives of the past and the articulation of narratives of responsibility that can be harnessed for other means of progressive politics. Moreover, autocritical memory's power was not in trying to search for ideal victims to celebrate and acknowledge in public (as laudable as this may be), but to face questions about what it means to address legacies of crimes beyond 'guilt'. In fragmented societies, it might just offer a way to articulate a future-oriented sense of responsibility that underpins a desire to 'move on' by accepting a past that cannot be changed.

Bibliography

Media

BBC Radio 4
Berliner Zeitung
Die Zeit
Frankfurter Allgemeine Zeitung
Frankfurter Rundschau
Gazeta Wyborcza
Głos
Le Monde
Nedeljni Telegraf
New York Times
Publico
Rzeczpospolita
The Guardian
The Herald
The Independent
The Observer
The Times
Washington Post
Wprost
Yorkshire Post
Życie

Oral history interviews

David Anderson, historian, Oxford, 16 October 2015.
Daniel Leader, Leigh & Day, London, 30.10.2015

Publications

Ackermann, Alice, 'Reconciliation as a Peace-Building Process in Post-War Europe: The Franco-German Case', *Peace and Change*, vol. 19, no. 3, 1994, pp. 229–50.

Adenauer, Konrad, 'Im deutschen Volk hat der Nationalsozialismus keine Wurzel', commemoration speech from 02.01.1960, *Bulletin des Presse- und*

Informationsamts der Bundesregierung, no. 11, published on 19 January 1960.

Adorno, Theodor, 'Kulturkritik und Gesellschaft', in Specht, Karl Gustav (ed.), *Soziologische Forschung in Unserer Zeit* (Wiesbaden: VS Verlag für Sozialwissenschaften, 1951), pp. 228–40.

Akala, *Natives: Race and Class in the Ruins of Empire* (London: Two Roads, 2019).

Amjahid, Mohamed, *Der weiße Fleck: Eine Anleitung zu antirassistischem Denken* (Munich: Piper, 2021).

Anderson, Benedict, *Imagined Communities: Reflections on the Origin and Spread of Nationalism* (London: Verso, 1991).

Anderson, David, *Histories of the Hanged: The Dirty War in Kenya and the End of Empire* (London: W.W.Norton, 2005).

Arendt, Hannah, 'The Aftermath of Nazi Rule from Germany', *Commentary*, vol. 10, 1950, pp. 342–53.

The Origins of Totalitarianism (New York: Schocken Books, 1951).

Eichmann in Jerusalem: A Report on the Banality of Evil (New York: Viking Press, 1963).

Arthur, Paige, 'How "Transitions" Reshaped Human Rights: A Conceptual History of Transitional Justice', *Human Rights Quarterly*, vol. 31, no. 2, May 2009, pp. 321–67.

Augé, Marc, *Les formes de l'oubli* (Paris: Payot et Rivages, 1998).

Augstein, Rudolf and Bracher, Karl Dietrich (eds.), *Historikerstreit: Die Dokumentation der Kontroverse* (Munich: Piper, 1987).

Aydemir, Fatma and Yaghoobifarah, Hengameh (eds.), *Eure Heimat ist unser Albtraum* (Berlin: Ullstein, 2019).

Baader, Meike Sophia and Freytag, Tatjana (eds.), *Erinnerungskulturen: Eine pädagogische und bildungspolitische Herausforderung* (Cologne: Böhlau, 2015).

Bach, Jonathan, *What Remains: Everyday Encounters with the Socialist Past in Germany* (New York: Columbia University Press, 2017).

Baer, Alejandro and Sznaider, Natan, *Memory and Forgetting in the Post-Holocaust Era: The Ethics of Never Again* (Abingdon: Routledge, 2019).

Baker, Catherine, *The Yugoslav Wars of the 1990s* (London: Bloomsbury, 2015).

Bass, Gary Jonathan, *Stay the Hand of Vengeance: The Politics of War Crime Tribunals* (Princeton, NJ: Princeton University Press, 2000).

Bennett, Huw, *Fighting the Mau Mau: The British Army and Counter-Insurgency in the Kenya Emergency* (Cambridge, MA: Cambridge University Press, 2013).

Bernhard, Michael, 'Democratic Backsliding in Poland and Hungary', *Slavic Review*, vol. 80, no. 3, (2021), pp. 585–607.

Bertrad, Romain, *Mémoires d'empire: La controverse autour du « fait colonial »* (Paris: editions du Croquant, 2006).

Błoński, Jan, 'Biedni Polacy patrzą na getto', *Tygodnik powszechny*, 1987/2.

Branche, Raphaëlle, *La Guerre d'Algérie, une histoire apaisée?* (Paris: Seuil, 2005).

Brandt, Willy, *Friedenspolitik in Europa* (Stuttgart: Verlag Deutscher Buchbund, 1970).

Brenner, Michael, *Nach dem Holocaust: Juden in Deutschland 1945–1950* (Munich: Beck, 1995).

Brusius, Mirjam, 'Das Humboldtforum ist nur der Anfang', in *Frankfurter Allgemeine Zeitung Feuilleton*, 28 September 2017.

Capdepón, Ulrike and Moses, Dirk (eds.), 'Forum: The Achille Mbembe Controversy and the German Debate about Antisemitism, Israel, and the Holocaust', special volume of the *Journal of Genocide Research*, vol. 23, no. 3, 2021, pp. 371–77.

Chabal, Emile, *A Divided Republic: Nation, State and Citizenship in Contemporary France* (Cambridge: Cambridge University Press, 2015).

Chirac, Jacques, *Allocution du Président de la République prononcée lors des cérémonies commémorant la grande rafle des 16 et 17 juillet 1942*, 16 July 2005, www.fondationshoah.org/sites/default/files/2017-04/Allocution-J-Chirac-Vel-dhiv-1995.pdf (last accessed on 23 February 2023).

Chivallon, Christine, *L'esclavage, du souvenir à la mémoire: Contribution à une anthropologie des Caraïbes* (Paris: Karthala, 2012).

Cohen, William B., 'The Sudden Memory of Torture: The Algerian War in French Discourse, 2000–2001', *French Politics, Culture & Society*, vol. 19, no. 3, 2001, pp. 82–94.

Cottias, Myriam, *La traite et les esclavages: Perspectives historiques et contemporains* (Paris: Karthala, 2010).

Crowe, David, *War Crimes, Genocide and Justice: A Global History* (London: Palgrave Macmillan, 2013).

Ćurgus Kazimir, Velimir, 'Jevreji, trgovke belim robljem i škorpioni', *Helsinška povelja*, vols. 83–84, 2005, pp. 26–8.

Cushman, Thomas and Mestrovic, Stjepan Gabriel, *This Time We Knew: Western Responses to Genocide in Bosnia* (New York: New York University Press, 1996).

Czollek, Max, *Desintegriert euch!* (Leipzig: Veltman, 2018).

David, Lea, *The Past Can't Heal Us: The Dangers of Mandating Memory in the Name of Human Rights* (Cambridge: Cambridge University Press, 2020a).

'The Emergence of the "Dealing with the Past" Agenda: Sociological Thoughts on Its Negative Impact on the Ground', *Modern Languages Open*, vol. 1, no. 19, 2020b. http://doi.org/10.3828/mlo.v0i0.321.

Del Ponte, Carla, *Madame Prosecutor: Confrontations with Humanity's Worst Criminals and the Culture of Impunity* (New York: Other Press, 2009).

Diallo, Rokhaya, *La France: Tu aimes ou tu la fermes?* (Paris: Textuel, 2019).

Diamond, Larry, 'Democracy's Third Wave Today', *Current History*, vol. 110, no. 739, November 2011, pp. 299–307.

Dimitrijević, Nenad, 'Serbia after the Criminal Past: What Went Wrong and What Should Be Done', *International and Transitional Justice*, vol. 2, no. 2, 2008, pp. 5–22.

Dresser, Madge, 'Remembering Slavery and Abolition in Bristol', *Abolition and Slavery*, vol. 30, no. 2, 2009, pp. 223–46.

Eddo-Lodge, Reni, *Why I'm No Longer Talking to White People about Race* (London: Bloomsbury Circus, 2017).

Eldridge, Claire, *From Empire to Exile: History and Memory within the Pied-noir and Harki Communities* (Manchester: Manchester University Press, 2016).

Elkins, Caroline, *Britain's Gulag: The Brutal End of Empire in Kenya* (London: Pimlico, 2005).

Fall, Rhodes Must, *Rhodes Must Fall: The Struggle to Decolonise the Racist Heart of Empire* (London: Zedd, 2018).

Ferdinand, Malcolm, *Decolonial Theory: Thinking from the Caribbean World* (Boston, MA: Polity, 2021).

Finchelstein, Federico, *The Ideological Origins of the Dirty War: Fascism, Populism and Dictatorship in Twentieth Century Argentina* (Oxford: Oxford University Press, 2014).

Fink, Carole and Schaefer, Bernd, *Ostpolitik, 1969–1974: European and Global Responses* (Cambridge: Cambridge University Press, 2009).

Florvil, Tiffany, *Mobilizing Black Germany: Afro-German Women and the Making of a Transnational Movement* (Champagne, IL: University of Illinois Press, 2020).

Foroutan, Naika, 'Neue Deutsche, Postmigranten und Bindungs-Identitäten: Wer gehört zum neuen Deutschland?' *Aus Politik und Zeitgeschichte*, vol. 46–7, 2010, pp. 9–15. http://doi.org/10.18452/21849.

Freud, Sigmund, *Zur Psychopathologie des Alltagslebens: Über Vergessen, Versprechen, Vergreifen, Aberglaube und Irrtum* (Frankfurt am Main: Fischer, ed. 2000).

Fritz Bauer Institut and Staatliches Museum Auschwitz-Birkenau (eds.), *Der Auschwitz-Prozess: Tonbandmitschnitte, Protokolle und Dokumente*, DVD (Frankfurt am Main: Directmedia, 2004).

Fukuyama, Francis, *The End of History and the Last Man* (New York: Free Press, 1992).

Gardner Feldman, L. 'The Principle and Practice of "Reconciliation" in German Foreign Policy: Relations with France, Israel, Poland and the Czech Republic', *International Affairs*, vol. 75, no. 2, 1999, pp. 333–56.

Gassert, Philipp, 'Die Klarsfeld-Ohrefeige', in Rösgen, Petra (ed.), *Skandale in Deutschland nach 1945* (Bonn: Haus der Geschichte, 2007), pp. 89–95.

Gensburger, Sarah and Lefranc, Sandrine, *A quoi servent les politiques de mémoire?* (Paris: Presses de Sciences Po, 2017).

Georgi, Viola B., Kahle, Lena, Freund, Sina Isabel and Wiezorek, Agata, 'Perspektiven von Lehrkräften: Migrationsgesellschaft, geschichtskultureller Wandel und historisches Lernen', in Georgi, Viola B., Lücke, Martin, Meyer-Hamme, Johannes and Spielhaus, Riem (eds.), *Geschichten im Wandel: Neue Perspektiven für die Erinnerungskultur in der Migrationsgesellschaft* (Bielefeld: transcript, 2012), pp. 61–123.

Goddereis, Idesbald, 'Black Lives Matter in Belgium (June 2020): A Catalyst in Postcolonial Memory?' *Rosa Luxemburg Stiftung, Brussels Office* (website), 6 October 2020, www.rosalux.eu/en/article/1796.black-lives-matter-in-belgium-june-july-2020.html (last accessed on 23 February 2023).

Goldmann, Nahum, *Mein Leben als deutscher Jude* (Munich: Langen Müller, 1980).

Gopal, Priyamvada, *Insurgent Empire: Anticolonial Resistance and British Dissent* (London: Verso, 2019).

Gross, Jan Tomasz, *Sąsiedzi: Historia zagłady żydowskiego miasteczka* (Warsaw: Fundacja pogranicze, 2000).

'Zrozumiałe morderstwo?' in *Gazeta Wyborcza*, 25–26 December 2000.

Habermas, Jürgen, 'Eine Art Schadensabwicklung: Die apologetischen Tendenzen in der deutschen Zeitgeschichtsschreibung', *Die Zeit*, 11 July 1986.

Hackmann, Jörg, 'Defending the "Good Name" of the Polish Nation: Politics of History as a Battlefield in Poland, 2015–18', *Journal of Genocide Research*, vol. 20, 2018, pp. 587–606.

Halbwachs, Maurice, *Les cadres sociaux de la mémoire*, 1st ed. (Paris: Presses universitaires de France, 1925).

La mémoire collective, 1st ed. (Paris: Presses universitaires de France, 1950).

Hammerstein, Katrin, Mählert, Ulrich, Trappe, Julie and Wolfrum, Edgar, 'Aufarbeitung der Diktatur – Diktat der Aufarbeitung? Normierungsprozesse beim Umgang mit diktatorischer Vergangenheit', in *Tagung 'Aufarbeitung der Diktatur – Diktat der Aufarbeitung'* (Göttingen: Wallstein, 2009).

Hans, Silke, 'Deutschland als Einwanderungsland', in Hans, Silke (eds.), *Assimilation oder Segregation?* (Wiesbaden: VS Verlag für Sozialwissenschaften, 2010), pp. 25–42.

Heitzer, Enrico, Jander, Martin, Poutrus, Patrice and Kahane, Anetta, *Nach Auschwitz: Plädoyer für einen Paradigmenwechsel in der DDR-Zeitgeschichtsforschung* (Frankfurt am Main: Wochenschau Verlag, 2018).

Herbst, Ludolf and Goschler, Constantin (eds.), *Wiedergutmachung in der Bundesrepublik Deutschland* special volume of the *Vierteljahresheft zur Zeitgeschite* (Munich: Institut für Zeitgeschichte, 1989).

Herf, Jeffrey, *Divided Memory: The Nazi Past in the Two Germanys* (Cambridge, MA: Harvard University Press, 1999).

Hirsch, Afua, *Brit(ish): On Race, Identity and Belonging* (London: Vintage, 2018).

Hobuß, Steffi, 'Mythos "Stunde Null"', in Fischer, Torben and Lorenz, Matthias (eds.), *'Lexikon der 'Vergangenheitsbewältigung' in Deutschland. Debatten- und Diskursgeschichte des Nationalsozialismus nach 1945* (Bielefeld: transcript, 2015), pp. 32–44.

Holesch, Adam and Kyriazi, Anna, 'Democratic Backsliding in the European Union: The Role of the Hungarian-Polish Coalition', *East European Politics*, vol. 38, no. 1, 2022, pp. 1–20.

House, Jim and MacMaster, Neil, *Paris 1961: Algerians, State Terror and Memory* (Oxford: Oxford University Press, 2006).

Jackson, Julian, *France: The Dark Years, 1940–1944* (Oxford: Oxford University Press, 2001).

Jackson, Julian, Milne, Anna-Louise and Williams, James S. (eds.), *May 1968: Rethinking France's Last Revolution* (London: Palgrave Macmillan, 2011).

Jaspers, Karl, *Die Schuldfrage* (Heidelberg: Lambert Schneider, 1946).

Jović, Dejan, *Rat i mit: Politika identiteta u suvremenoj Hrvatskoj* (Zaprešić: Faktura, 2017).

Kahveci, Çağri, 'Transversale Politik des Antirassimus und Antifaschismus?' in Nobrega, Suzan Onur, Quent, Matthias and Zipf, Jonas (eds.), *Rassismus. Macht. Vergessen. Von München über den NSU bis Hanau: Symbolische und materielle Kämpfe entlang rechten Terrors* (Bielefeld: transcript, 2021), pp. 219–32.

Kedward, Rod, *Occupied France: Collaboration and Resistance, 1940–1944* (London: John Wiley and Sons, 1985).

The French Resistance and Its Legacy (London: Bloomsbury, 2022).

Klimke, Martin and Mausbach, Wilfried, 'Auf der äußeren Linie der Befreiungskriege: Die RAF und der Vietnamkonflikt', in Kraushaar, Wolfgang, Die RAF und der linke Terrorismus (Hamburg: Hamburger Edition, 2006), pp. 620–43.

Kößler, Reinhart, *Namibia and Germany: Negotiating the Past* (Münster: Westfälisches Dampfboot, 2015).

Kößler, Reinhart and Melber, Henning, *Völkermord – und was dann? Die Politik deutsch-namibischer Vergangenheitsbearbeitung* (Frankfurt am Main: Brandes & Apsel Verlag, 2017).

Kraushaar, Wolfgang, *1968 als Mythos, Chiffre und Zäsur* (Hamburg: Hamburger Edition, 2002).

Kraushaar, Wolfgang (ed.), *Die RAF und der linke Terrorismus* (Hamburg: Hamburger Editionen, 2006).

Kritz, Neil, *Transitional Justice: How Emerging Democracies Reckon with Former Regimes* (Washington, DC: United States Institute of Peace Press, 1995).

Ledoux, Sébastien, 'Silence et oubli de la mémoire de la Shoah: une « illusion » historiographique?', *En Jeu, Revue pluridisciplinaire de la fondation pour la mémoire de la déportation*, vol. 2, December 2013, pp. 76–93.

Le Devoir de mémoire: une formule et son histoire (Paris: Editions CNRS, 2016).

'Des « origines » du « devoir de mémoire » aux sources de la mémoire de la Shoah: historiciser la mémoire de son oubli', *Les Cahiers de FRAMESPA* (open access), vol. 41, 2022. https://journals.openedition.org/framespa/13398 (last accessed on 23 February 2023).

Liauzu, Claude and Mançeron, Gilles (eds.), *La colonisation, la loi et l'histoire* (Paris: Syllepse, 2006).

Lindlar, Ludger, *Das mißverstandene Wirtschaftswunder: Westdeutschland und die westeuropäische Nachkriegsprosperität* (Tübingen: Mohr Siebeck, 1997).

Lotem, Itay, 'Anti-racist Activism and the Memory of Colonialism: Race as Republican Critique after 2005', *Modern and Contemporary France*, vol. 24, no. 3, 2016, pp. 283–98.

'Between Resistance and the State: Caribbean Activism and the Invention of a National Memory of Slavery in France', *French Politics, Culture & Society*, vol. 36, no. 2, 2018, pp. 126–48.

The Memory of Colonialism in Britain and France: The Sins of Silence (London: Palgrave Macmillan, 2021).

Lotem, Itay, 'The Road to 2005: How the Memory of Colonialism in France Became a Substitute for Race', in Chafer, Tony and Majumdar, Margaret (eds.), *The Routledge Handbook of Francophone Africa* (Abingdon: Routledge, 2023), pp. 324–39.

Löytömäki, Stiina, 'The Law and Collective Memory of Colonialism: France and the Case of "Belated" Transitional Justice', *International Journal of Transitional Justice*, vol. 7, no. 2, 2013, pp. 205–23.

Lübbe, Hermann, *Die Aufdringlichkeit der Geschichte: Herausforderungen der Moderne vom Historismus bis zum Nationalsozialismus* (Graz: Styria, 1989).

Macierewicz, Antoni, 'Rewolucja nihilizmu', in *Głos*, 3 February 2001.

Messerschmidt, Astrid, 'Geschichtsbewusstsein ohne Identitätsbesetzungen – kritische Gedenkstättenpädagogik in der Migrationsgesellschaft', *Aus Politik und Zeitgeschichte*, vol. 66, no. 3–4, 2016, pp. 16–22.

Michlic, Joanna Beata, *Coming to Terms with the 'Dark Past': The Polish Debate about the Jedwabne Massacre* (Jerusalem: Vidal Sassoon International Center for the Study of Antisemitism, The Hebrew University of Jerusalem, 2002).

Miller, Barbara, *The Stasi Files Unveiled* (Abingdon: Routledge, 2017).

Misztal, Barbara, *Theories of Social Remembering* (Maidenhead: City University Press, 2003).

Mitscherlich, Alexander and Mitscherlich, Margarete, *Die Unfähigkeit zu trauern: Grundlagen kollektiven Verhaltens* (Munich: Piper, 1967).

Moller, Sabine, Tschuggnall, Karoline and Welzer, Harald, *'Opa war kein Nazi': Nationalsozialismus und Holocaust im Familiengedächtnis* (Frankfurt am Main: S. Fischer, 2002).

Möller, Kurt, Grote, Janne, Nolde, Kai and Schumacher, Nils, *'Die kann ich nicht ab!' – Ablehnung, Diskriminierung und Gewalt bei Jugendlichen in der (Post-) Migrationsgesellschaft* (Cham: Springer Verlag, 2016).

Moses, Dirk, 'Der Katechismus der Deutschen', 21 May 2021. https://geschich tedergegenwart.ch/der-katechismus-der-deutschen/ (last accessed on 16 February 2023).

Mouralis, Guillaume, 'The Invention of "Transitional Justice" in the 1990s', in Israël, Liora and Mouralis, Guillaume (eds.), *Dealing with Wars and Dictatorships: Legal Concepts and Categories in Action* (The Hague: TMC Asser Press, 2014), pp. 83–100.

Mouvement the Indigènes de la République, *Appel des Indigènes de la République*, 10 January 2005. https://indigenes-republique.fr/le-p-i-r/ appel-des-indigenes-de-la-republique/ (last accessed 16 February 2023).

Moyn, Samuel, *The Last Utopia: Human Rights in History* (Cambridge, MA: The Belknap Press, 2012).

Musiał, Bogdan, 'Nie wolno się bać', *Życie*, 2 February 2001.

Neiman, Susan, *Learning from the Germans: Race and the Memory of Evil* (New York: Farrar, Straus and Giroux, 2019).

Obradović-Wochnik, Jelena, 'The "Silent Dilemma" of Transitional Justice: Silencing and Coming to Terms with the Past in Serbia', *International Journal of Transitional Justice*, vol. 7, no. 2, July 2013, pp. 328–47.

Olsen, Tricia, Payne, Leigh and Reiter, Andrew, 'Demand for Justice: Domestic Support for Transitional Justice Mechanisms' (paper presented at the Annual Convention of the International Studies Association, San Francisco, CA, March 26–9, 2008).

Olusoga, David, *Black and British: A Forgotten History* (London: Pan, 2017).

Olusoga, David, 'The Toppling of Edward Colston's Statue Is Not an Attack on History: It Is History', in *The Guardian*, 8 June 2020.

Özcan, Ertekin, *Türkische Immigsrantenorganisationen in der Bundesrepublik Deutschland* (Berlin: Hitit, 1989).

Paxton, Robert, *Vichy France: Old Guard and New Order 1940–1944* (New York: W. W. Norton, 1972).

Peskin, Victor, *International Justice in Rwanda and the Balkans* (Cambridge, MA: Cambridge University Press, 2008).

Piatkowski, Marcin, *Poland's New Golden Age: Shifting from Europe's Periphery to Its Centre*, Report submitted for World Bank Policy Research Working Papers, October, 2013.

Prochasson, Christophe, *L'Empire des émotions: Les Historiens dans la mêlée* (Paris: DEMOPOLIS, 2008).

Prošić-Dvornic, Mirjana, 'Serbia: The Inside Story', in Halpern, Joel and Kidecker, David (eds.), *Neighbors at War: Anthropological Perspectives on Yugoslav Ethnicity, Culture, and History* (University Park, PA: Pennsylvenia University Press, 2000), pp. 317–38.

Radović, Bratislav, 'Yugoslav Wars and Some of Their Social Consequences', in Špiric, Željko, Kneževic, Goran, Jović, Vladimir and Opačić, Goran (eds.), *Torture in War: Consequences and Rehabilitation of Victims: Yugoslav Experience* (Belgrade: IAD, 2004), pp. 25–68.

Rai, Rohini and Campion, Karis, 'Decoding "Decoloniality" in the Academy: Tensions and Challenges in "Decolonising" as a "New" Language and Praxis in British History and Geography', *Ethnic and Racial Studies*, vol. 45, no. 16, 2022, pp. 478–500.

Reichel, Peter, *Vergangenheitsbewältigung in Deutschland: Die Auseinander-setzung mit der NS-Diktatur von 1945 bis heute* (Munich: C. H. Beck, 2001).

Ricoeur, Paul, *La mémoire, l'histoire, l'oubli* (Paris: Le Seuil, 2000).

Rosoux, Valérie, 'La réconciliation franco-allemande: crédibilité et exemplarité d'un « couple à toute épreuve » ?' *Cahiers d'histoire: Revue d'histoire critique*, vol. 100, 1 January 2007, pp. 23–36.

Rothberg, Michael, *Multidirectional Memory: Remembering the Holocaust in the Age of Decolonization* (Stanford, CA: Stanford University Press, 2009).

Rousso, Henry, *Le Syndrome de Vichy de 1944 à nos jours* (Paris: Seuil, 1987).

Sarr, Felwine and Savoy, Bénédicte, *Rapport sur la restitution du patrimoine-culturel africain: Vers une nouvelle éthique relationnelle*, 2018, http://restitutionreport2018.com/.

Schildt, Axel, *Rebellion und Reform: Die Bundesrepublik der Sechzigerjahre* (Bonn: Bundeszentrale für politische Bildung, 2005).

Schönwälder, Karen, 'Migration und Ausländerpolitik in der Bundesrepublik Deutschland Öffentliche Debatten und politische Entscheidungen', in Beier-deHaan, Rosemarei (ed.), *Zuwanderungsland Deutschland: Migrationen 1500–2005* (Berlin: Deutsches Historisches Museum, 2005), pp. 106–19.

Sontheimer, Kurt, 'Gegen den Mythos von 1968', *Die Zeit*, 8 February 2001.

Soroka, George and Krawatzek, Felix, 'Nationalism, Democracy, and Memory Laws', *Journal of Democracy*, vol. 30, no. 2, April 2019, pp. 157–71.

Stora, Benjamin, *La gangrène et l'oubli: La mémoire de la guerre d'Algérie* (Paris: La Découverte, 1991).

Stora, Benjamin, *Le Transfert d'une mémoire: de l'Algérie française au racisme anti-arabe* (Paris: La Découverte, 1999).

Les guerres sans fin, un historien entre la France et l'Algérie (Paris: Stock, 2008).

Rapport: Les questions mémorielles portant sur la colonisation et la Guerre d'Algérie, 2021, https://medias.vie-publique.fr/data_storage_s3/rapport/pdf/278186.pdf.

Strzembosz, Tomasz, 'Z jednej okupacji pod drugą', *Rzeczpospolita*, 28 July 2001.

Subotić, Jelena, *Hijacked Justice: Dealing with the Past in the Balkans* (Ithaka, NY: Cornell University Press, 2009).

'The Cruelty of False Remorse: Biljana Plavšić at the Hague', *Southeastern Europe*, vol. 36, 2012, pp. 39–59.

Suckut, Siegfried and Weber, Jürgen, *Stasi-Akten zwischen Politik und Zeitgeschichte: Eine Zwischenbilanz* (Munich: Olzog, 2003).

Teitel, Ruti, *Transitional Justice* (Oxford: Oxford University Press, 2001).

Todzi, Kim and Zimmerer, Jürgen, *Hamburg: Tor zur kolonialen Welt: Erinnerungsorte der (post-)kolonialen Globalisierung* (Göttingen: Wallstein, 2021).

Törnquist-Plewa, Barbara, 'The Jewdwabne Killings: A Challenge for Polish Collective Memory', in Karlsson, Klas-Göran and Zander, Ulf (eds.), *Echoes of the Holocaust: Cultures in Contemporary Europe* (Falun: Nordic Academic Press, 2003), pp. 141–74.

Trouillot, Michel-Rolph, *Silencing the Past: Power and the Production of History* (Boston, MA: Beacon Press, 1995).

Von Weizsäker, Richard, *Rede zur Gedenkveranstaltung im Plenarsaal des Deutschen Bundestages zum 40. Jahrestag des Endes des Zweiten Weltkrieges in Europa*, Bonn, 8 May 1985, www.bundespraesident.de/Shared Docs/Reden/DE/Richard-von-Weizsaecker/Reden/1985/05/19850508_Rede .html (Last accessed on 23 February 2023).

Wieviorka, Annette, *L'Ère du témoin* (Paris: Hachette, 2002).

Déportation et génocide: Entre la mémoire et l'oubli (Paris: Hachette, 2003).

Winkler, Heinrich August, *Der lange Weg nach Westen. Deutsche Geschichte II. Vom 'Dritten Reich' bis zur Wiedervereinigung* (Munich: C. H. Beck, 2014).

Wolf, Joan, *Harnessing the Holocaust: The Politics of Memory in France* (Stanford, CA: Stanford University Press, 2004).

Wood, Nancy, *Vectors of Memory: Legacies of Trauma in Postwar Europe* (London: Bloomsbury, 1999).

Younge, Gary, 'Why Every Statue Should Come Down', in *The Guardian*, 1 June 2021.

Zajak, Sabrina, Sommer, Moritz and Steinhilper, Elias, 'Black Lives Matter in Europa – Antirassistischer Protest in Deutschland, Italien, Dänemark und Polen im Vergleich', *Forschungsjournal Soziale Bewegungen*, vol. 34, no. 2, 2021, pp. 319–25.

Zimmerer, Jürgen, 'Die Geburt des "Ostlandes" aus dem Geiste des Kolonialismus: Ein postkolonialer Blick auf die NS-Eroberungs- und Vernichtungspolitik', *Sozial.Geschichte. Zeitschrift für die historische Analyse des 20. und 21. Jahrhunderts*, vol. 1, 2004, pp. 10–43.

Von Windhuk nach Auschwitz? Beiträge zum Verhältnis von Kolonialismus und Holocaust (Münster: LIT Verlag, 2011).

'Der Kolonialismus ist kein Spiel', in *Frankfurter Allgemeine Zeitung*, 9 August 2017.

Zimmerer, Jürgen and Zeller, Joachim (eds.), *Völkermord in Deutsch-Südwestafrika: Der Kolonialkrieg (1904–1908) in Namibia und seine Folgen* (Berlin: Ch. Links Verlag, 2003).

Acknowledgements

This is a concise element, and I will therefore keep my thanks short and sweet. This Element would not have seen the light of day without the support of the following people (in no specific order of appearance): Daniel Woolf, Charlotte Faucher, Blake Smith, Claire Eldridge, Rebecca Infield, Noëmie Duhaut, Gerda Wielander, Debra Kelly, Rachael Attwood, Siavash Bakhtiar, Lucia Llano-Puertas, Dragana Stojanović, Ed Naylor, Natalya Vince, Elsa Peralta, Inês Nascimento Rodrigues, Christoph Kalter, Julian Jackson, Henna Patel, Justin Colson, Rebekah Vince, Johannes Becker, Jessica Pearson, Anne Stenvot, Kathleen Gransow, Hélène Tiard, Frank Mikus, Stephan Schmuck, Miri Stryjan, and (not least) Christian Arndt.

Cambridge Elements ≡

Historical Theory and Practice

Daniel Woolf
Queen's University, Ontario

Daniel Woolf is Professor of History at Queen's University, where he served for ten years as Principal and Vice-Chancellor, and has held academic appointments at a number of Canadian universities. He is the author or editor of several books and articles on the history of historical thought and writing, and on early modern British intellectual history, including most recently *A Concise History of History* (CUP 2019). He is a Fellow of the Royal Historical Society, the Royal Society of Canada, and the Society of Antiquaries of London. He is married with 3 adult children.

About the Series
Cambridge Elements in Historical Theory and Practice is a series intended for a wide range of students, scholars, and others whose interests involve engagement with the past. Topics include the theoretical, ethical, and philosophical issues involved in doing history, the interconnections between history and other disciplines and questions of method, and the application of historical knowledge to contemporary global and social issues such as climate change, reconciliation and justice, heritage, and identity politics.

Cambridge Elements ☰

Historical Theory and Practice

Elements in the Series

A full series listing is available at: www.cambridge.org/EHTP

Printed in the United States
by Baker & Taylor Publisher Services